Dedicated to the memories of
Mrs Adora Brown
and
Mrs Joyce Louise Mullings,
veterans of the faith!

LIST OF ACRONYMS, SPECIAL FEATURES, AND TERMINOLOGIES

His—Appears in this form throughout this book when used as a pronoun referring to the Sovereign Lord God. The idea of showing reverence to the Lord God is one of the intentions we hope to convey. We believe that by doing this, we are helping to promote the distinction between the Lord God and any other person to whom, or thing to which, the usage of this pronoun may apply.

Minister (Ministerial)—Used as a proper noun throughout this book when referring to the Minister's office and those who serve to demonstrate its significance.

Ministry—Presented in this form throughout this book to demonstrate its corresponding importance to the Minister. It is the office of the Minister to which it is referring and not the activities of ministry that is in view.

BSMoS—An acronym which stands for *Biblical Spiritual Model of Supervision*. In chapter 4 of this book, I use this acronym for ease of writing and quick reference for the reader.

Footnotes—I have used footnotes throughout this book to recognise the various publications cited in its construction. I believe it allows for easy reference and that it also serves to encourage the reader to undertake further exploration, should interest increase while reading this book.

CONTENTS

PREFACE

The conviction to undertake the writing of this book (learning resource) initially came about while Bishop Crentsil Manful, the national overseer of Church of God Ghana, prayed over the lives of the mission team of 2018 at the point of our departure from Kumasi to Accra. He prayed, giving thanks to God for what He had placed in us to share with the people we encountered and fellowshipped with for the two weeks we had been serving alongside his team. I sensed the appeal of the Holy Spirit as he prayed to give focused attention to the idea of capacity expansion and development. Later that same day, I understood this to be a personal message, so I decided not to share it with the team. I kept it to myself and pondered the level of commitment it would demand and what new and exciting revelations would generate from engaging with such a theme for me and those I serve within the Ministry.

I was distressed and conflicted between the conviction of the Holy Spirit and my natural need for rest. However, the need for clarity pressed deeply upon me. I could not silence the voice of the Holy Spirit within me even though I wished to give my attention to another matter, which I felt to be of greater importance at the time. I wanted to rest my mind and my body because I was exhausted from the intensive work we had to do and did not think that I had the physical or mental energy to give reasonable time to meditate on what I heard. However, the specific thought about capacity expansion did not let go of me!

After saying our goodbyes, we boarded our bus where Brother Amos, a very godly and noble Ghanaian man, awaited to take us to our Accra destination. Within minutes of the journey, I fell asleep. I awoke sometime later to discover that we were still in Kumasi, parked in the courtyard of a petrol station with several people attending to our transportation radiator, which was leaking. Everyone else had already departed the bus, so I too alighted and went browsing in the petrol station's shopping area. I noticed a bookstand as I came to the checkout counter to pay for some drinks I had taken from the cooler. One of the books caught my attention: John C. Maxwell's *No Limits: Blow the Top Off Your Capacity*. I picked it up, examined it for its publication date, and checked its contents for themes and subthemes. I remember pausing and thinking, *Lord, is this a confirmation that I need to write about capacity expansion?*

Without hesitation I purchased the book, re-entered the bus, and started reading it. To date, I have only read the first couple of pages on the subject of awareness. I stopped reading because of the spiritual conviction on my heart about writing what is now in your hands. I felt that the Spirit wanted me to write outside of the influence of Maxwell's work. Therefore, I heeded and pledged that I would not read what he wrote until after completing what I feel was an assignment given by the Holy Spirit.

I realised the Holy Spirit used the occasion of the prayer service and John Maxwell's book to convince me that I should write on the subject of capacity expansion and development. I perceived this would contribute to my personal and ministerial growth and development. Additionally, I understood it would be an essential resource for supporting others to grow and develop their God-given capacities.

I honoured the Holy Spirit's conviction and set about writing down initial thoughts and ideas as they came to mind. It has taken just over one year to complete this book (training resource). I had hoped to spend less time on it, but when I became unwell with depressive feelings in late November 2018 when I engaged in a prolonged period of reflecting on my earlier years, I left it with no thought of ever returning to it. However, the Holy Spirit ministered to me through gifted holy men and women. I recovered and was able to give devotional attention to it. I have much to account for concerning the difficulties experienced throughout the process of writing this book. I have even more for which to give thanks and praise to God. He sustained me to complete this assignment and to triumph over the powers of darkness that tested me.

The production of this book has been a real challenge for me in many respects. The first has to do with the expansion and development of my capacity and the place I stand to write what may seem to be a directive given to others. As I grappled with this challenge, I considered the various implications for me as a Minister of the Gospel of the Lord Jesus Christ. I have come to a place of tentative rest in the knowledge that it is from the perspective of a developing practitioner from whom these feeble words go and not from one "who has already attained ... or already perfected" (Phil. 3:12). I am still seeking through conversations with others—both small and great—but more so, through time with the Word and prayer to grow and develop the capacity I received from the Lord. Through the practice of such spiritual disciplines, I will gain a more in-depth understanding, greater wisdom, and more robust courage to more fully hone the capacity bestowed upon me by God.

Fighting against the temptation to become content with the level of capacity expansion attained over the years seems to be a challenge I must manage consistently. I can confidently say that this is a battle I am winning through the knowledge that the Holy Spirit continues to reveal to my mind concerning the more profound depths and higher heights in Christ Jesus to discover and enjoy. Upon realising the fact of "the unsearchable riches of Christ" and "the fellowship of the mystery" hidden in God (Eph. 3:8–9), I am persuaded to "press toward the goal for the prize of the upward call of God in Christ Jesus" (Phil. 3:14). For me, this goal constitutes a great deal more than being in heaven and enjoying all the fantastic things provided there for the redeemed.

Discovering the height and the depth, the length and breadth of the love of God (Eph. 3:18), and the strategies and skills required for its diffusion amongst human communities is a part of the understanding I hold regarding the goal which God has called me to achieve in Christ. In pursuit of this noble goal, I am learning about God—Father, Son, and Holy Spirit—in a way that demands and facilitates actual conformity to His image in Jesus Christ (Rom. 8:29). Importantly, I discovered that such compliance should be possible by following the example of Jesus's condescension to the will of God to take unto Himself the fragility of humanity (John 1:14, 18; Phil. 2:5–8). Besides, I recognised and accepted Jesus's sacrificial self-giving, which demonstrates most correctly the love of God for a world ravaged and defaced by sin and divine judgement (John 3:14–17, 10:11; Gen. 3:1–19) as critical to conforming to the image of God in Jesus Christ. Like Jesus, I too must embrace humanity in all its weakness so that I may also know, amidst the heat of service to the weak and the poor, the full measure of the dynamic might of the Holy Spirit who lives with me (Rom. 12:1–8; Acts 1:8).

Growing the capacity, which the Lord has bestowed upon me, has been quite a challenge. Having to contend with the world, the flesh, and the devil presents a problem for which only those who have the power of the life and love of God can sufficiently overcome (Rom. 8:31–39). Learning to walk in step with the Holy Spirit (Gal. 5:16) even as He guides into the right path (John 16:13) can be a real challenge when carnal desires crave prominence and priority. My father and teachers had frequently told me I would never amount to anything of worth.

Others remarked that my place in the world was predetermined by the abject poverty of the socio-economic context in which I was born. These statements left me intellectually and emotionally disabled for many years. Such negativity left me living with crippling self-doubt and low self-esteem, from which God delivered me. I still experience difficulties with such negativity, even now that the Holy Spirit lives in me and actively administers love and hope within me. Although I am now more aware of the beautiful and vital existence for which God created and redeemed me (Gen. 1:26–28; 1 Pet. 2:9–10), these negative pronouncements can result in debilitating self-fulfilling prophecies if I am not vigilant. These are some of the hazards I must continually wrestle with and resist, because they try to attack my mind without notice and respite, if allowed.

But thanks to God for His persistent healing and unconditional love, the journey for me has become more comfortable. Now, I am allowing myself to receive, believe, and appropriate the many precious promises God gave concerning my place of significance in Jesus's Church (Matt. 16:18; 1 Cor. 1:2; Eph. 1:22–23, 4:11–13). I am pressing forward in the adventure of discovering and expanding the capacity which the Lord bestows upon me. I am reaching for the upward calling of God in Christ Jesus (Phil. 3:14) with the expectation of positively affecting the lives of many people for the glory of His name.

I have come to accept that the production of this book is in fact a vital means by which my capacity for reflection and writing, besides other essential skills, can grow and develop. The ideas and thoughts contained in this book were birthed and clarified through prayer, reading, and meditation on the Word of God, as well as moments spent in conversations with the great and the small, I encountered in life. I came to realise that I have acquired a deeper understanding of the vital aspects of my capacity while affording opportunities for the development of such precious souls through the engaging and invaluable processes in which I participated with them.

Another challenge I had is that which pertains to the actual voice in which I was to write this book. By voice, I mean the authorship of the work. I fully accept that I am an instrument of God in the production of this book, but I am also very conscious of the Holy Spirit's inspiration, which is the most invaluable ingredient in its realisation. The countless other human channels through which I have received great insight and encouragement deserve this book's co-authorship. They gave out of their wisdom and knowledge, gained through lived experiences in the power of the Holy Spirit, and have significantly contributed to what is now a vital product that will benefit many souls for God's ultimate glory. As a result of such realisations, I chose to write in the collective voice, *we*. This collective *we* is intended to give recognition to the many unnamed heroes and heroines of the faith, whose contributions have helped to add immeasurable value to my growth and development and the content of this book.

As I have benefited greatly from the time spent writing this book, I hope you will also find help even as you give yourself time and space to read and reflect on its contents. I hope you will make favourable decisions to embrace and practise the all-important revelations, the critical principles, and the vital insights outlined in these pages. If your walk of faith and the particular capacity you have received from the Lord is positively affected in the least, then the energies expended in writing this book would be correctly invested.

Barrington A. Mullings

FOREWORD

It is a privilege to commend this learning resource.

Drawing from his pilgrimage, Barrington Mullings appeals to Ministers to take responsibility for their growth and development in Christian leadership. His depth of biblical knowledge, spiritual insights, pastoral sensitivity, teaching expertise, and desire to help men and women lead with integrity can be heard loud and clear throughout the chapters.

He presents convincing reasons for teaching and learning for growth in discipleship and leadership roles. Besides, he provides strategies and tools for those motivated by the aspiration to mature in their authenticity as disciples of Jesus with reputable credibility in their practice of ministry.

Barrington Mullings writes authoritatively and passionately to equip leaders with the means to critically reflect on their abilities and aptitude and adopt the necessary self-discipline to engage in intentional learning to enable the move from good to better, and from better to best, in their leadership roles. His premise is rooted in biblical theology and transformational theory. This learning material offers a well-considered guide to those engaged in Christian ministry. It signposts indicators of clear vision and presents effective strategies to facilitate what he calls capacity expansion and development. He is of the view that effective ministers are those who understand ministry as a process of becoming. Becoming proficient dispensers of divine grace, underpinned with intentional learning strategies for capacity expansion as agents of God's grace to enable more significant outcomes in biblical spiritual ministries, is both a goal and a process. His sobering claim that "the objective is not to find fault but to offer support where required" is evident in his choice of approach, techniques, and language.

The material is comfortably challenging. It invites the learner to explore scripture, discover what it has to say about the Spirit-led leader in pursuit of excellence for kingdom purposes, and use the tools offered to develop the requisite discipline for growth and maturity in Christian leadership.

This work is an excellent contribution to the collection of ministerial learning resources. It is suitable for the training of leaders across the denominational streams and global contexts. To this end, I expect the School of Ministerial Excellence to grow from strength to strength and become a prominent point of reference for many Christian leaders.

Rev. Phyllis Thompson
M.Ed., EQUIP Certified Trainer
Author and Educator
Former Education Director for New Testament
Church of God United Kingdom
July 2020

CITATIONS FOR
Capacity Expansion and Development

"In *Capacity Expansion and Development*, Barrington Mullings challenges the reader and the church to push beyond their self-imposed boundaries, and to discover the potential to which they are called in Christ. He underlines the fact that many of our limitations and our boundaries are self-imposed because we expect so little of ourselves and of God and fail to take into consideration the power of the Holy Spirit.

The book begins by reminding the reader that "the discipleship journey is one of growth and development, and one to which the Spirit calls all followers of Jesus Christ." The Church and the Christian must resist the temptation to assume that they have exhausted their potential – whatever their age, their education, their background, their place in life, their personal history.

Barrington explores key passages of scripture, pursuing the idea, in Old Testament and New, that there is a recurrent theme reminding us to allow God to show us the potential of our calling in Christ. From God's purpose in creation, to Christ's example in incarnation, to the lessons of the Epistles, scripture is examined to point to God's plan for the church and for Christians.

Barrington helpfully takes time throughout his book to call us to reflect and respond, with exercises for reading, meditation, and self-examination, at each stage of his work. This offers the reader an opportunity to consider how each section might be applied in her or his own life.

But this is not only a theoretical examination of a scriptural exhortation: Barrington takes time to examine strategies for identifying and developing one's spiritual capacities: the importance of finding time for reading;

the primacy of prayer; the overlooked gift of peer development; and the benefits of mentorship and supervision.

This is a call to 'release the handbrake' on our spiritual lives: to recognise the vast, untapped potential within the church, and so within our own lives."

— **Dr Peter Rea, PhD**
Academic Dean
Nazarene Theological College – Manchester UK

"This book is a 'must-have' resource for leaders and laity who are striving to increase their capacity for the more profound things of God in their effort to lead His people. Bishop Mullings writes out of his passion and draws from his depth of experience in Church leadership to offer some well-considered practical guidance for trainers of leaders of churches though not exclusively so. He itemises disciplines and intentional growth plans for success in the training of leaders such as intimacy with the triune God, prayer, rigorous study of scripture and other literature, peer conversations and supervision. I genuinely believe this training resource will enable the achievement of the intended learning outcomes. Therefore, I highly recommend it to all who wish to make a positive impact in the lives of those they lead for our common good and bring about God's kingdom on earth as it is in heaven."

— **Dr Donald Bolt**
Administrative Bishop
New Testament Church of God England and Wales

ACKNOWLEDGEMENTS

Many people deserve heartfelt acknowledgement and appreciation for the production of this book. Though I do not intend to overlook anyone, there is a strong likelihood that I am not able to identify everyone deserving of praise for their invaluable contribution to the production of this book. I acknowledge with sincere appreciation the unsung heroes and heroines whose prayers and words of encouragement provided much-needed inspiration and motivation. Yours is a share of the joy which this book produces in countless numbers of lives. Your happiness will be increased not just for the production of this book but also for the immeasurable positive impact it will achieve amongst the rank and file of Christian leaders and the communities they serve for the glory of God.

I wish to give special recognition and thanks to Mrs Patsy Mackie. The gift you gave me ten years ago served as an investment and a motivation that kept me honest and loyal to the conviction I shared—that God has blessed me with the ability to write books for Christian development and the glory of His name. Thank you for recognising the capacity which God bestowed upon me and the faith you demonstrated by investing in its development.

A special note of appreciation goes out to Dr Roy Notice for the timely challenge and needful provocation he issued when he responded to my query about him writing and publishing with, "Where is your publication?" This question provoked a process of reflection that resulted in valuable discoveries for which this book represents a fraction.

Heartfelt appreciation goes out to Mrs Claire Wharton, who read the manuscript and provided necessary corrections that significantly improved its quality. However, the prayers you offered on my behalf provided a more lasting impact, in that they secured the release of God's special anointing that contributes greatly to the development of my capacity.

Rev. Michael Bradley, I appreciate you for the time you took to read the manuscript and for the invaluable discussions we have had about some of its central themes. They enriched me, and the content of the book was dramatically enhanced as a result.

A special thank-you goes to my dear brother, Jonathan Stubb who did the final proofing of the manuscript, even when he experienced health challenges. I will always remember your sacrifice!

It is to Kemar Jackson that I offer heart-felt gratitude for bringing such beauty to this invaluable work by producing the book cover. This is a work of art designed to inspire generations! Your sacrifice is greatly appreciated.

To my dear wife, Maxine, and my children, Romona and Joel, I thank you for the many sacrifices you have made and the encouragement and love you gave me over the process of writing this book. These gifts have brought me through difficult moments and helped me overcome the temptation to give up midstream.

It is to God—Father, Son, and Holy Spirit—that I offer my most profound appreciation and highest praise for having considered me a valued partner in producing this book, which He inspired for personal and communal capacity expansion and development.

CHAPTER 1

The Word of God: Believers' Source of Light and Life

Counselling helps people work on their weaknesses. Equipping helps people work on their strengths … We all need the help of someone else to become aware of how to become better at reaching our capacity.[1]

Introduction

Countless people have come to accept the Bible as the Word of God and have given it a high priority in their lives. The Bible is reported to be "the best-selling book of all time with an estimated 5 billion copies sold and distributed."[2] This level of popularity attests to the value of the claims that the Bible makes of its contents. In effect, it is to enable success and prosperity that God's Word is given (Josh. 1:8).

The enlightening character of God's Word is one of the motifs that the Bible uses to promote its critical importance amidst human communities. God's Word is presented "as a lamp" for the feet and "a light" that enlightens

[1] John C. Maxwell, *No Limits: Blow the Cap Off Your Capacity* (New York: Centre Street, 2017), 3–4.

[2] Wikipedia, "List of Best-Selling Books," https://en.wikipedia.org/wiki/List_of_best-selling_books.

the path of the righteous; it also gives "understanding to the simple" (Psa. 119:105, 130).

Isaiah, the prophet of Jehovah God, speaks about God's Word as possessing an enduring character (Isa. 40:8) and its instinctive prosperity disposition (Isa. 55:10–11). The apostle Paul promotes in Romans 10:14–17 this instinctive prosperity motif of the Word of God as the very means by which saving faith is produced in the hearts of those who would come to believe in God and share in His glorious salvation. Besides, the productive imagery of the Word of God is promoted in Hebrews 4:12. In this text, the Word is presented to all people as God's "mighty worker"—dissecting, discerning, healing and holding people accountable. It was on the strength of such convincing evidence that Paul wrote the following to his mentee, Timothy:

> All Scripture is given by inspiration of God, and is profitable for doctrine, for reproof, for correction, for instruction in righteousness, that the man of God maybe complete, thoroughly equipped for every good work. (2 Tim. 3:16–17)

The vitality of God's Word in human living and serving is outlined above for everyone whose hands this book has come to consider intentionally. The indispensable value of God's Word is presented above not just to promote its necessity for faith and salvation but also to highlight the adversity of darkness, ignorance, sickness, and death that is likely should it be rejected. Hebrews 2:1–4 warns against dismissing the Word that God's Son brings to humanity by drawing attention to previous examples of Israel's rejection of God's Word and the destruction they attracted.

Given such realisation, we aim to sketch a striking parallel between Israel's diminishing capacity for God's Word and the current state of affairs with Christians, particularly those who occupy leadership roles in Christian ministries and communities. We intend to demonstrate that rejecting the Word of God leads to divine judgment in whatever context or era people may live. This parallelism is drawn to provoke a more incredible passion for more in-depth knowledge of God's Word in the interest of expanding and developing bestowed capacity for achieving more substantial and enduring outcomes in biblical spiritual ministries.

1. The Peril of a Stagnant and Diminishing Capacity in the Knowledge of God's Word

The prophet Hosea cited the Children of Israel's diminishing capacity in the knowledge of the Lord God Jehovah as the cause of the frequent episodes of socio-economic unrest they experienced throughout their history. The prophet's actual declaration was more empathic and gruesome than the insights or inferences purported in the sentence above. A more accurate rendering of the Old Testament text brings into full focus the deadly consequence of spiritual stagnation and the counterproductive disposition which characterised the lives of those who reject the knowledge of God. "My people are destroyed because of a lack of knowledge. Because you have rejected knowledge, I also will reject you from being priests for Me; because you have forsaken the laws of your God, I will also forget your children" (Hos. 4:6).

The content of Hosea 4:6 carries the emphatic message of generational destruction concerning all who would treat the revealed knowledge (word) of God with disdain. At the heart of this message lies the thought that failure to thrive in the knowledge of God constitutes a specific pathway to poverty and destruction. Interestingly, this lack of spiritual striving is about the flagrant disregard that God's covenant people intentionally direct against the vital truths He offers for communal edification, spiritual envisioning, clarification of purpose, and empowerment for the execution of responsibilities intrinsic to their composition. Furthermore, a failure to thrive in the knowledge of God is an inadvertent rejection of God's good plans for the holistic development of the people He sanctified to share in covenant relationship with Himself. Social and economic advancement, physical longevity, and the promotion of God's redemptive endeavours amongst the nations (Gen. 12:1–3; Deut. 8:3; Josh. 1:8–9; Ps. 1:1–6; Matt. 5:13–16) are significant aspects of the salvation plan that is forfeited whenever people reject the knowledge of God.

One of the two crucial insights that Hosea's declaration suggests is the solemn and sobering fact that it is never good enough to just believe in God and Jesus Christ. Faith in God and Jesus Christ is more than an intellectual exercise. At its core lies its dynamic values which consummate in the holistic transformation of those who would come to trust God through faith in Jesus Christ for salvation. Being transformed by the power of faith in Jesus Christ transcends social reformation. This is the case because believing in Jesus Christ engenders a radical transformation of an individual's faculty (Rom. 12:1–2). Partaking of God's life and serving the purpose of the heavenly kingdom in partnership with Him (John 1:12–13; Matt. 11:28–30; Acts 1:8; Eph. 2:10) are critical aspects of the consummative work of authentic biblical faith in the soul of believing humanity. These vital spiritual graces are the inevitable outcomes for all who come to God through faith in Jesus Christ, primarily because faith is a product of the dynamic, life-giving, creative Word of God (Rom. 10:17; Heb. 4:12). Therefore, to have confidence in Jesus Christ is to share His life and to desire the things of God (Col. 3:1–4). To assent to faith in Jesus Christ merely as an intellectual exercise is to be like the devil in disposition and works, focusing only on worldly things that will eventually perish (James 2:19; 1 John 2:15–17).

The second insight that Hosea's declaration brings to mind is that the destruction that is encountered comes about because of believers' wilful rejection of life-giving truths and the abandonment of the presence of God. The message of God that the prophet announced speaks not just to Israel's rejection of God's Word; it also reveals the frightening fact of God's temporary abandonment of His people. The inevitable consequence of death and destruction whenever life-giving truths are rejected advertises an indisputable logic that no reasonable person could contest. It should be expected that to refuse light in a dark world is to seal one's fate. Failure to value the light-generating Word of God contributes to spiritual blindness and its effects amongst the people of Israel (Jer. 25:1–11; Hos. 4:1–10), the religious people who lived during the first century AD (Matt. 23:16–22; Act 4:7:51–53), and Christian disciples of the current era.[3]

The idea of divine abandonment may appear to be quite stark and devoid of compassion. However, it shows the seriousness of the divine intention when it comes to the value of the Word. The implicit stringency of Hosea 4:6 should be seen in its universal appeal and intent, not as a statement limited to the specific and restrictive historical context to God's dealings with the nation of Israel. Romans 1:16–32 provides evidence of the universal application of God's willingness to abandon all who would trifle with and reject His Word. This revelation brings to our awareness of how intricately linked God is to

---

[3]   Ronald J. Sider, *The Scandal of the Evangelical Conscience* (Grand Rapids, MI: Baker, 2005).

His Word and that a rejection of His Word is tantamount to rejecting Him. Believers should never be ignorant of the intimate relationship between God and His Word, primarily because the Holy Scriptures speak directly to this fact. (See, for example, Isa. 55:10–11 and John 1:1–3.)

Israel's mode of operation is a template for understanding how believers should live in a postmodern society. Neglecting God's revealed will has left church communities more affected by underdevelopment than by the gates of hell. Whilst Jesus declares that the "gates of hell shall not prevail against" the Church that He is building (Matt. 16:18), the lives of many believers seem to attest more to the works of the gates of hell and less to the power of Jesus. The positive message of the prevailing character of Jesus's Church and the definite demise of the brutal works of the kingdom of darkness are rich with hope and assurance for every believer. However, many have not yet learned to walk in the victory and prosperity intrinsic to this announcement. This state of affairs, which is the generally lived reality of many who claim association with the Lord Jesus Christ and His Church, is predicated on the practice of rejecting the Word of God (Eph. 2:2). This activity of rejecting God's Word is not a new thing but one that has plagued humanity since that fateful occasion in the Garden of Eden (Gen. 3:1–6; cf. Gen. 2:16–17). The antithesis of the blessed man or woman in Psalm one, which continues to demonstrate the portrayal of rebelliousness as sketched by the content of Genesis 3, is that of the perishing person who is a rejector of the Word of God.

What, then, might be the hindrance to the blessings which are promised to us by the Living God? With humility and a persistent desire to be of service for the good of all believers, we propose that one of the critical reasons for the prominence of failings, distress, and bondage amongst many believers is the combination of a weak spiritual mentality and its corresponding carnal behavioural deportment. The frivolous attitude showed towards the gift of grace God generously bestowed renders believers vulnerable and ineffective before the tempter. An inferior understanding of the basics of the faith results in various behavioural displays which contravene biblical spirituality.

This practice of rejecting God's Word gives rise to empty prayers and unfulfilled expectations that leave believers and the watching world wondering about the authenticity of the faith we confess. A stagnant or diminishing capacity in the Word of God is the primary cause of the ignorance which believers demonstrate about the spiritual blessings which God has generously supplied. This ignorance, above all else, has caused much suffering for the body of Christ on earth.

Seducing spirits have deceived many church attendees in believing that to commit the written Word of God to memory, or having it tattooed on their bodies or written on their clothes and other personal properties (Deut. 6:6–9), is the totality of what believers need to do to cultivate intimacy with God. Such is the effect of the work of deceiving spirits amongst believers that the ability to memorise and quote key scripture texts is given a more prominent position in Christian churches above encountering the Holy Spirit of the Word (John 6:63). But genuine spiritual intimacy that produces God's life in the human soul comes when the Word of God is carved in the inner heart by the Spirit (Jer. 31:33). This miracle is about mutual abiding— the Word dwelling in believers and believers dwelling in the Word—by the work of the indwelling Spirit (John 15:1–8). This mutual abiding is a mystery and a miracle which God accomplishes by the Holy Spirit in the life of people who surrender themselves to Him through faith in Jesus Christ.

Hosea's lamentation rings true in the now as it had at the very instance when he opened his mouth to speak via the inspiration of the Lord's Spirit. Spiritual stagnation and underdevelopment of spiritual gifts are two of the root causes of the cry of despair and distress that continues to echo above the hymns of promise and praise we religiously sing in our erected cathedrals. This hopelessness and suffering persist primarily because many disciples of Jesus have not realised the essential developmental feature of God's grace.

The failure of many believers to see God's gift of grace as expansive has led to the underdevelopment of countless numbers of gifted individuals and many vital ministries in the Church. As a direct result, many gifts have not been developed to their fullest extent or used to their most significant potential. This underdevelopment of spiritual gifts has, in turn, affected the quality of the faith of many individuals and the ministry operations of entire congregations. The distressing accounts of ministerial misconduct with the particular features of power and sexual abuse accounted for in David Johnson and Jeff Van Vonderen's book *The Subtle Power of Spiritual Abuse*[4] speak to the fact of the reductionist theology that has become the

---

[4]   David Johnson and Jeff Van Vonderen, *The Subtle Power of Spiritual Abuse* (Minneapolis: Bethany House, 1991).

bedrock of many postmodern church communities in the United States. Kathy Galloway and David Gamble's revealing work, *Time for Action*,[5] exposes the sexual violence and abuse of power which are very much endemic in Christian communities in the United Kingdom. In many sectors of secular society, the Church appears to have very little to offer concerning current debates on gender reassignment, the redefinition of marriage, and other political operations. Moral turpitude, social disconnections, and the unrelenting economic exploitation of those relegated to society's fringes persist without any concerted redress from those occupying the corridors of power within the Church. This silence continues primarily because reductionist ideologies have mostly replaced the core values that distinguished the Apostolic Church of the first century AD. At the same time, there is the emergence of a theological conservatism that appears to be academically shy. While it advertises itself as Pentecostal, the dynamic, inspirational, and revolutionary operations of the Spirit, which are both expansive and progressive, appear to be absent from the witness that the Church is currently delivering within the marketplace of the world.

Such concerns may have been uppermost in Paul's mind when he directed believers residing in the city of Rome to confine their thinking and their subsequent ministry function to the measure of grace which God gave them (<u>Rom. 12:3–8</u>). Although Paul's guidance seems restrictive in its appearance, his intention was not to prevent development and expansion in the ministry capacity of divinely endowed servants. The substance of the text is about partnership ministry operation and the implicit reciprocal respect accorded to each Minister of grace within their specific area of service. Capacity restriction and spiritual stagnation are not the intended message of the passage. Therefore, believers must vehemently oppose any idea or notion that appears to lean towards spiritual underdevelopment and ministerial stagnation. This resistance is a duty that Ministers of grace must discharge irrespective of the source from which such corrupting ideas come. The responsibility to oppose corrupters of the faith should not be ignored or neglected. Because the ideas they promote are restrictive in their intention, debilitating in their nature, and destructive in their operational

---

5   Kathy Galloway and David Gamble, *Time for Action: Sexual Abuse, the Churches, and a New Dawn for Survivors* (London: Churches Together in Britain and Ireland, 2002).

character, Ministers of grace should be vigilant and fervent in resisting them, in defence of the faith (Jude 3). To be coy with the proposers of such deadly ideas is to run the risk of unleashing the virus of heresy amongst the Church of the Lord Jesus Christ. We must resist this in the strength of the revelations which we obtain through contemplative praying and protected time in the Word.

We believe every disciple of Jesus will benefit in some way from this book. However, it is established Ministers of grace and those emerging from the communities we are familiar with whom we call to engage with its contents. This invitation to expand and develop personal capacities for victorious living and effectiveness in service is the clarion call located at the heart of Hosea 4:6. My heart's plea is that the Ministers I encountered in the mission field in the United Kingdom, Jamaica, and Ghana who are more concerned with acquiring money and status would take heed to Hosea's message and become pursuers of God and His Word instead. Realising the diminishing prestige of things, in the light of the glory "of the upward call of God in Christ Jesus" (Phil. 3:14), can only lead to expanding and developing bestowed capacities amongst Ministers of grace and an aversion of the dreadful judgment contained in Hosea's prophecy. As Ministers of grace become more ardent in pursuing fellowship with God and His Word, in the Spirit, those who benefit from such ministry will live for the salvation of the unsaved and the glory of God (Matt. 5: 13–16).

2. Key Aims and Objectives

In response to the various concerns highlighted above, we pray that this work will generate amongst spiritual leaders, discussions that focus on some generally misinterpreted and misapplied concepts such as capacity, expansion, and development. Because they have negatively affected the growth and developmental opportunities that are made possible through the Holy Spirit's leading, addressing them within a context that endeavours to promote spiritual excellence through prayerful exploration in the Word of God, is the responsible thing to do. This hope constitutes the first of the three key aims of this work. We anticipate that everyone who engages in this reflective exercise challenge will come to recognise that capacity growth and development are expected outcomes for all who participate in the vital and necessary discipleship programme outlined in the scriptures. The discipleship journey is one of growth and development, and one to which the Spirit calls all followers of Jesus Christ (Matt. 16:23–24; John 8:31–32; Eph. 4:11–16). As a central part of every Christian's calling, growth and development through discipleship are not something we can afford to ignore. Ignoring this call of the Spirit leads to stagnation and ineffectiveness of the individual believer and the Church. Holistic growth and development are vital characteristics that the Spirit expects each member of the body of Jesus Christ to demonstrate throughout their lives and in keeping with the expansive nature of the life of Jesus (Isa. 9:6–7) which we share in the Spirit (Rom. 8:9–11). Discussions that allow for mutual sharing and the challenge to strive for excellence, which is conformity to the image of God in Christ Jesus, constitute an essential means of facilitating the growth and development most urgently required among followers of Jesus Christ.

Exploring some of the vital teachings presented in the scriptures regarding the expansive and developmental nature of the capacities received from the Lord as properties of the redemption He affords us (John 1:12–13; 2 Cor. 5:17; Phil. 2:1–2) is the second of the primary aims of this book. We hope that this will provide the valuable theological understanding and compelling motivation for all who participate in this program of study to become more intentional and purposeful in endeavours to expand and develop the capacities received from the Lord. In effect, this commitment is expected to result in growth and development that produces more exceptional outcomes in the respective services we are currently offering. We may find ourselves developing interests and desires in new areas of service even as our capacity stretches through the expansion and development exercises we undertake. Equally, we may become more streamlined in our work for the kingdom as new and deeper spiritual direction provides a more intense joy in service and an uneclipsed focus for Ministry. Therefore, we should be open to the possibility of change as we undertake this journey in our discipleship pathway. Established Ministers should desire a more precise understanding of the vital capacities received through God's bestowed grace and be willing to demonstrate the same before emerging leaders. While this will accentuate the value of living for the salvation of other human beings and God's glory, it will also establish the process as a standard of critical importance in capacity expansion and development. A commitment to this aspect of the Ministry can only encourage a more profound sense of curiosity amongst younger disciples to explore, discover, and commit to the specific missionary objectives which the Holy Spirit pursues in the world today.

Identifying and reflecting on additional capacity expansion and development strategies, such as reflection, supervision, and peer conversation, is also an essential aim of this work. We think it is particularly important to highlight these strategies for expanding and developing divinely bestowed capacities because they are not generally promoted amongst many Pentecostals as necessary and vital to spiritual growth and effectiveness in ministry. Although much talking happens in collegial circles, anecdotal stories of conflict, burnout, pastoral failings, relationship challenges, and family breakdown are telltale signs of the contents of such talk. But the production of vital knowledge collated and presented for the dual purpose of accounting for the positive changes and transformation affected amongst those engaged in such conversations and of being a reservoir from which emerging leaders can draw inspiration and example is still absent. The impact of this is evident when considering the accountability and supervision structures of some of the United Kingdom's black-majority churches, such as the New Testament Church of God (NTCG).[6] This church organisation has no enforceable, established supervision policy that focuses on Ministerial accountability, opportunity for critical Ministry review, and Ministerial holistic growth and development.

This issue extends beyond the typical lack of formal accountability and supervision policies, manifesting in a reluctance to engage in formal theological study opportunities. The absence of a robust internal ministerial regulation process results in the minimal utilisation by serving Ministers of the study opportunities that the NTCG provides for spiritual enrichment and ministerial development through its Leadership Training Centre (LTC) and its Annual Oliver Lyseight lectures. Doubtless, this has reduced effectiveness in pulpit ministry, the counselling room, and the many other areas where services are delivered. Sadly, this has been one

---

[6]   Specifically, the absence of a statement which accounts for the importance of ministerial supervision as a formalised process that is undertaken for personal development and safeguarding of persons who are involved in the delivery of ministry in the NTCG's Administrative Governance Manual (2014).

reason for the increasing disconnection of many young and intellectually gifted believers—potential leaders, emerging theologians, and Ministers—from the established Church. Engagement in the vital growth and developmental strategies indicated above could produce the kind of results that demonstrate why our Church has been allowed to exist in the world.

In addition to the three broad aims collated in Figure 1.1, we hope that the vital knowledge and unique insights that everyone will gain through the contents of this book will help them

- become more acutely aware of the capacity that has been bestowed to them by the Lord God, through faith in Jesus Christ, by the Holy Spirit;
- recognise and accept the responsibility for the expansion of divinely bestowed capacity for maximised operation in the Church of Jesus Christ; and
- identify pathways through which divinely bestowed capacity can be developed, increased, and enhanced in its composition to greater effectiveness in service and higher production in fruit-bearing.

Figure 1.1

**Capacity Growth and Development
Aims to Be Achieved**

- To generate discussions amongst spiritual leaders that focus attention on some generally misinterpreted and misapplied concepts such as capacity, expansion, and development, which have negatively affected the growth and developmental opportunities that are made possible through the Holy Spirit.
- To explore some of the vital teachings presented in the inspired scriptures regarding the expansive and developmental nature of the capacities received from the Lord as properties of the redemption He affords us.
- To identify and reflect on additional capacity expansion and development strategies, such as reflection, supervision, and peer-conversation.

We designed these aims to provide much more than an outline against which to assess the logic and substance of the information contained in this book. The production of this book was not an intellectual exercise that stopped with any challenge that its contents may yield. Challenging prevailing attitudes and perceptions about bestowed spiritual capacity, its growth and development, and its intending purpose amongst believers and the people of the world is a goal that we would be pleased to have accomplished. The actual process of growing and developing our capacities for measurable outcomes in Ministry was at the very heart of the production of this book.

3. Initial Capacity Assessment

Before embarking on a more in-depth exploration of capacity expansion, in the subsequent chapter, it is worth taking some time to reflect on your current understanding of capacity at this juncture. We ask that you use the Capacity Assessment Grid (Figure 1.2) to aid your reflection. The idea for this learning aid evolved through time spent in meditation and facilitating conversations with fellow believers on subjects pertinent to self-development and pastoral care service. We noticed that the process of using various questions to interrogate the topic or theme occupying our focus generated critical information that deepened understanding and aided development and productivity. We are confident that this task will offer much more than an intellectual exercise.

Your experience is likely to change during your study, but it can be quite beneficial to take stock at the beginning of the exercise. This exercise in reflection should be an opportunity to recognise and affirm your discipleship journey thus far while allowing you to identify areas for personal growth and development. It is also an excellent opportunity to engage early on with one of the critical strategies proposed in this work for capacity expansion and development, especially because many may be unfamiliar with the practice of self-reflection, as noted above. Therefore, we consider that it is essential to take time at this early point to reflect and evaluate your current understanding, and hopefully to come to recognise self-reflection as a meaningful and significant aspect of our discipleship journey with the Sovereign God. We cannot overemphasise the importance of engaging in an exercise of reflection of this nature. We are not seeking to make a case for this faith expansion strategy, because it is one that is already established by men of renown since ancient times. The place of prominence King David gave to the practice of reflection (Ps. 1:3, 8:3–9) illustrates its critical importance in facilitating capacity growth and development in the lives of God's ministering servants. The quality of the service he rendered to Israel is not the only measurement that we could use to evaluate the extent of his legacy for which time spent in reflection has contributed significantly. Solomon's writings, particularly the book of Proverbs, attest to the value of meditation in King David's life (Prov. 4:3–9).

Yet a perfect example of the practice of reflection is offered to us by Jesus Christ. He would rise early in the morning or withdraw from the bustling and demanding crowds to be alone in the presence of the Father (Mark 1:35; Luke 5:16). As the One who received the Spirit without measure found value in time spent reflecting in the presence of the Father, we who are dependent on Him for light and life (John 1:2) and access to the Father (John 14:6) cannot do less!

Some may find our rendering of Jesus in communion with the Father as reflection somewhat unusual because the mode of praying many disciples witnessed within our church tradition is extemporaneous. Perhaps this feature of our faith practice has never been formally taught or explored as a reflective process even though that is what we do when we make supplications, petitions, and intercessions for others and ourselves regarding our encounters and lived experiences. Principally, reflection is what we do whenever we give ourselves time to consider the particular set of circumstances we have experienced throughout our Christian pilgrimage. But the value of this reflection is enhanced during time spent reading the Word of God. Our prayers, which are generally composed of requests for God's intervention in our lives— and where such intervention would bring to realisation the liberating and enriching substance of the promises in which our hope stand—are intrinsically reflective.

Allowing time to reflect about capacity at this early stage will enable us to become more aware of how we view ourselves and our abilities. This knowledge is invaluable and should not be neglected or treated as inconsequential to personal growth and development as persons of significance called from the world of sin and darkness into partnership with the Sovereign God (John 14:23; Acts 1:8; 1 Cor. 3:9; Eph. 2:10). We are unable to enumerate the possible benefits to be gained from this exercise. Only the personal evaluation of our participation in doing it will yield such results. Therefore, please consider the following seven questions and then document your responses to each of them in their corresponding spaces.

No.	Questions	Personal Responses
Figure 1:2 **Capacity Assessment Grid**		
1.	How do you understand the term *capacity* concerning Christian discipleship and Ministry?	
2.	What capacity do you think you have?	
3.	Do you believe that your capacity is limited? If so, in what ways?	
4.	Can capacity be increased? If so, what might you need to do to achieve this?	
5.	Whose responsibility is it to increase your capacity?	
6.	How might age be a factor in the increase or decrease in the capacity that a person has?	
7.	In your understanding, does capacity have a singular or a multidimensional structure? Please explain your answer.	

4. Personal Expectation Grid

Engaging with the subject of this book requires much more than a blasé attitude. Such an attitude should be treated disdainfully by every child of God because its very presence contradicts the fact that we are children of God (John 1:12–13), God's new creation (2 Cor. 5:17), and the efficacy of the Spirit who guides us "into all truth" (John 16:13). The demand for a commitment that is rooted in faith is what is required. Anything less is a waste of time. Curiosity is not what we intend to evoke in the minds of the established and emerging spiritual leaders that we appeal to through these pages. Expanding and developing the capacities which God bestowed for affecting changes that outlast our physical existence requires spiritual leaders to possess an intentional and sacrificial disposition. At the heart of this book lies an expectation of the emergence of a body of people who will significantly impact the world at large through biblical spiritual ministries for the glory of God– Father, Son, and Holy Spirit.

The writer of the epistle to the Hebrews declared that it is impossible to please God without faith, for all who come to Him "must believe that He is and that He is the rewarder of those who diligently seek Him" (Heb. 11:6). Expectation based upon God's identity and ability is one of the many insights to be grasped from this verse. What we do in study and service should also be underlined with great expectations because we live and serve with the Spirit, in constant pursuit of conformity to the image of God as revealed in Jesus Christ.

The idea of expectation is vilified in certain circles because it is associated with disappointment. The desire attached to the famous proverb "Blessed is he who expects nothing, for he shall never be disappointed"[7] is one that promotes the shirking of responsibilities. It also undermines progress and prosperity and encourages slothfulness and promotes mediocrity.

However, the teaching Jesus gave about responsibility and expectation in Luke 12:35–48 counters the notion of sailing through life without expectations. He has spoken definitively: "For everyone to whom much is given, from him will much be required; and to whom much has been committed, of him they will ask the more" (Luke 12:48b). Followers of Christ cannot journey through life without expectations. He expects each

---

[7] John Simpson, *The Oxford Library of Words and Phrases, Vol. II: Proverbs* (London: BCA, 1982), 20.

of us to deliver in accord with the capacity that we have received. He also directs us to have expectations of each other based on the grace that we have received. In light of such revelations, we believe you have come to this book with some expectations of your own.

Therefore, as with the previous exercise, we consider it beneficial to reflect on your expectations before going further with this study. Take some time to consider the aims listed earlier and your answers to the capacity assessment exercise. Reflect on what you hope to gain from this study and how you hope it will impact your discipleship journey and your current ministry. This exercise can help you to engage with this course of study on a deeper level as you recognise the personal expectations with which you approach it. The answers to this exercise can also serve as a consequent basis of reflection at the end of the study, allowing you to reflect on where you do end up, compared with where you thought you would.

Personal Expectations
1)
2)
3)
4)
5)
6)
7)

CHAPTER 2

Defining the Concepts
Capacity and Expansion

Transformation enforces hope. It is what is needed in our town halls, community projects and parliaments.[8]

Introduction

This chapter's primary role is to offer a definition of capacity and consider what capacity expansion, as a spiritual reality, could mean for all who are a part of Jesus's Church. The insight gained from exploring capacity's working definition will provide the framework for moving forward and help shape the discussions around capacity expansion. We hope that the exploration of capacity expansion will highlight its crucial importance in the life of every follower of the Lord Jesus Christ. The intention is to point everyone towards some possible avenues, through which the expected increase and development of God's bestowed grace gets realised for enabling all to grow in their journey of discipleship.

Before we get to this chapter's main substance, we think it is necessary to shed light on the decision we have made concerning how to use the terms *expansion* and *development* throughout this work. They are used to

---

8   Joel Edwards, *An Agenda for Change* (Grand Rapids, MI: Zondervan, 2008), 101.

indicate two distinct facets of capacity instead of interchangeable terms, so explaining the reasons for this decision is as important as what we have to say about how they contribute to growing the abilities that God bestows for living and serving in His kingdom.

1. Expansion and Development as Nuances of Capacity

The terms *expansion* and *development* may be used interchangeably to speak to the dynamic reality of growth or productivity. However, we have decided to treat them as separate terms within the scope of this book. We based this decision on the view that *expansion* and *development* can mean different things and, as such, should be considered as different aspects of growth, particularly as they relate to the subject of capacity. We believe that expansion does not necessarily mean the same as development and vice versa, even though both terms contribute to a more in-depth understanding of capacity.

For example, Ministers could expand their knowledge of a particular subject yet fail to demonstrate the efficacy of what has been committed to memory. While they have participated in accumulating new information and may reproduce the same when prompted, they do not actively apply their new learning as development in their character or practice of ministry. Being able to recount concepts and ideas in a conversation does not equate to development. For growth to be registered as a factor of importance in a possible learning experience for Ministers, they need to demonstrate how the content of their education has positively informed and affected personal attitudes towards life and service. Contributing to improving particular modes of operation in some, if not every aspect of their ministry and their effectiveness in service, is critical in evidencing personal, professional, and ministerial development.

The example discussed above highlights two crucial points that explain why we have decided to treat expansion and development as separate entities and facets of growth instead of treating them as synonyms. The first critical point concerns the fact that Ministers have grown in their understanding of a particular subject's technical knowledge and have become able to converse intelligently about its contents. However, this growth is minimal and ineffective in the dynamic spiritual operation of the Church if it offers nothing of substance that demonstrates measurable outcomes, in terms of positive character changes and improved engagement in ministry.

Second, development as a holistic enterprise inclusive of the acquisition of knowledge and its actual application to lived experiences that are both observable and measurable is wholly different from a mere accumulation and re-presentation of information. Improvement in ministry practice and the achievement of ministry objectives are two factors of every learning experience that are consistent with a holistic and positive understanding of growth and development. It is not only the context of formal education or planned study that afford growth and development for disciples of Jesus Christ. Every aspect of life, every situation encountered, and every experience (both negative and positive) can contribute to the growth and development of Christian disciples. Everything counts! This holistic approach to learning and development is the declaration of scripture (Rom. 8:28–29; 1 Thess. 5:18), which informs the attitudes we have concerning all we encounter and experience in life.

Our responses to all that we tend to label negative and positive, good and evil, should be identical primarily because they all work for our good, as ordained by God. This knowledge, and the understanding it seeks to produce, is critical to each believer's holistic health, and it also constitutes a necessary weapon in our warfare against the wicked one. Possessing and operating in this knowledge nullifies the spirit of fear and depression whenever we face life's challenges. It also informs our prayers and prevents us from wasting time and energy, considering why we have become subject to whatever we face. As recorded in Psalm 23, King David's testimony offers evidence of the integrity of this truth, which we would do well to have and to hold. In it, he celebrates God's abiding presence and the faithfulness of His preserving love and miraculous provisions. The gifts of grace he received resulted from having walked the path in which the Spirit led him in faith.

Celebrating in worship before the presence of the Lord, despite trials and tribulations, is expected when we know that the Lord orders our steps. Should we fail to trust the Lord's providential power and purpose for our lives, we may very well end up like the children of Israel in the wilderness of Zin, wandering in circles and having nothing to speak about besides complaints and a pining desire for a former existence of oppression (Exod. 1:1–18, 15:22–27, 16:1–3, 17:1–3, 32:1–35; Num. 11:1–6, 13:31–33, 14:1–10, 26–38).

Increasing the volume of information or wealth that a person possesses can lead to other things besides positive development. At times, the possession of information and ideas can lead to pride, arrogance, selfishness, oppression, depression, and the demise of self and others. These adverse situations may have been what King David endeavoured to highlight when he gave this warning to his readers: "Do not trust in oppression, nor vainly hope in robbery; if riches increase, do not set your heart on them" (Ps. 62:10). Importantly, it is not the gift or the position received that should hold the attention of the people of God. When this happens, idolatry and self-defeat are the only results achieved. Ministers of grace can avert the pit of false worship when their thinking and affection are of the Lord and the purposes for which He gave His disciples gifts (Eph. 4:11–16; 1 Pet. 4:7–11). Whenever Ministers of grace attain this level of understanding about spiritual gifts, worship and service are the inevitable outcomes. It is this place of knowledge and humility that we should conscientiously and intentionally strive to occupy before the presence of the Lord. This particular spiritual disposition causes us to assume a platform of service from which we serve all humankind for the glory of God. However, if the effects of the increase experienced, whether in knowledge or wealth, were the collective improvement of others as directed respectively by Paul in 1 Corinthians 12:7 and James in James 1:22–27, then development would have most certainly been achieved.

Given the possibility of such subtle variances, treating *expansion* and *development* as separate entities can help us develop more comprehensive knowledge regarding what is possible in exploring capacity expansion and development.

2. Defining the Concept of Capacity

Collins English Dictionary offers ten different definitions for the noun *capacity*. The first five are adopted and used in this book primarily because the remaining five are mere extensions of the first five, in that they are used to sketch the broad spectrum of its application. The following are the five selected for our reflection and learning.

1. The ability or power to contain, absorb, or hold
2. The amount that can be contained; volume
3. The maximum amount something can contain or absorb

4. The ability to understand and learn; aptitude; capability
5. The ability to do or produce[9]

We have identified four key themes from the five definitions of capacity. These themes, which offer some invaluable insights about capacity, are explored later. They are essential thoughts, which are useful to help us critically assess how we customarily viewed capacity as a unique and prominent feature of importance within the context of our faith and its intrinsic spiritual services.

The first theme identified is that which points to the fact that capacity is about ability and power. These two words speak to the idea of capacity as being dynamic. The apparent dynamic feature of ability and power is one that is both expandable and impactful. We know this to be true, in that ability can grow and mature even as power can become more significant in its influence and impact. Increase and expansion are very much vital aspects of the nature of what constitutes ability and power. Therefore, capacity is both functional and far-reaching in its strength and impact. This evident expansion is very much in accord with the definitions presented above. The vital question that we must now answer in the light of such valuable insights is this: To what extent have the ability and power components of the capacity we received from the Lord grown over the last decade? We need to answer this question in two ways. First, we need to provide an answer that will demonstrate how the gifts we received from the Lord have developed over the years since we have come to God through faith in Christ Jesus by the Spirit. The knowledge gained from being in a relationship with the Trinity should help us account for our impact among those we serve what we have received from the Lord.

The second theme evident from the above definitions of capacity is the available volume for absorption and containment. Despite the usage of the term *containment*, one should not interpret this to mean restriction, as in the case of suppression. The intention that we seek to express here focuses on the maximum amount of resource that can be absorbed or contained in the particular receptacle that is in view. Therefore, this theme implies three things that are of vital importance to Christian disciples. The first relates to storage potential, the second is concerned with the principle of retention, and the third has to do with the actual resource stored.

---

9   *Collins English Dictionary, Seventh Edition* (Glasgow: HarperCollins, 2008), 250.

We understand the volume capacity that we possess as believers can be a genuinely revolutionising experience for Christian living and serving. Realising that the space we have for the reception of bestowed grace is stored in Christ and accessible through the Spirit by faith, is most reassuring and empowering (1 Cor. 2:9–16; Eph. 1:3–6). All is not dependent upon our commitment to studying and committing the scriptures' vital truths to memory, even though these are encouraged as spiritual disciplines that believers should make established life habits (Josh. 1:8; Ps. 1:1–3; 2 Tim. 2:15). It is not within the human memory that the vital substance of divinely bestowed capacities is stored. Within the mind of the Spirit, we find sufficient space for receiving the grace which God gave to His children. It is within the depths of the Spirit who regenerates that the available volume for absorption and containment is stored. By pairing this theme with the first one, this critical question arises: What is the volume of ability and power within the capacity that we each possess as children of God? Finding answers to this question might be the key required for a revival the likes of which the world has never seen.

Growth in understanding is the third theme we detected from the definitions of capacity presented earlier. This theme also implies the possibility of growth and expansion. Understanding can be limited or restricted depending on exposure, knowledge, experience, and opportunity. However, wherever these features are present, growth and development in understanding are inevitable for Christian disciples and should be expected. One of the many important questions that this theme raises for us is, What is our level of understanding of the capacity we have received from the Lord, and how should we utilise it in offering service to the members of the body of Christ and the unsaved masses of the world?

One word comprises the fourth theme drawn from the above five definitions of capacity: productivity. The other components we examined so far express the conventional idea of dynamism, which speaks to the value of productivity. Power and ability, volume for absorbing containment, and growth in understanding, are all themes of vitality. Because vitality is another important word that offers additional insights about productivity, there is no surprise to find that the fourth theme in our exploration of capacity is productivity.

From the suggested sequential structure that the components of capacity forms, we can conclude that it is directional in its dynamic nature.

It does not only provide power and ability, with volume for absorbing containment and understanding, but it is also productive in the fullness of its manifestation. Capacity produces much, thus impacting situations and individuals and bringing about evident and measurable change by its various dynamic components. Because of such intense vitality, this is the all-important question that we need to answer: What apparent changes in our relationships and the community where we live and serve can we attribute to the capacity we have received from the Lord?

Given the four underlying themes derived from the five definitions of capacity, we understand that capacity is not a one-dimensional concept. It has many components, each of which offers something of vital importance to its overall operational integrity. This understanding of the multidimensional nature of capacity is what permeates the content of this book. Therefore, wherever the term *capacity* appears in this book, we suggest that you give attention to its multifaceted nature for your personal, professional, and ministry appraisal. By doing this, you will become engaged in a learning experience that allows for the affirmation of everyone you encounter as persons of worth and significance, while growing and developing holistically in personhood, ministry understanding, effectiveness in serving people's natural, and spiritual welfare—all for the ultimate glory of God.

Figure 2.1
Components of Capacity: A Scriptural Measurement

- **Capacity is about power and ability**—effective influence:
  - These are bestowed to believers by God through the Holy Spirit.
  - Acts 1:8; Rom. 12:3–8; 1 Cor. 12:7–11; Eph. 4:11–16

- **Available volume and absorbing containment**—expansive storage:
  - Becoming children of God fits us with an enormous capacity to receive and absorb all that the Father has willed for us.
  - Rom. 5:8; Eph. 1:3, 3:20–21

- **Growth in understanding**—insightfulness and tactical applicability:
  - Expanding in the knowledge of God and God's kingdom, in which He calls believers to become citizens, is an expectation that the Godhead has of every believer.
  - John 16:13–16; 1 Cor. 2:9–12; 1 Pet. 3:18

- **Productivity**—effective impact, fruitfulness:
  - Believers' lives and ministry are to produce positive impact, irrespective of the context in which they live and serve.
  - Positive impact: Matt. 5:6, 28:19–20; John 15:8
  - Negative impact: Matt. 5:11–12; John 15:18–25; 1 Pet. 4:1–4

3. Exploring the Concept of Expansion

The noun *expansion* speaks about "the act of expanding or the state of being expanded."[10] The first part of this definition addresses development as a process, and the second part focuses on the extent of the actual expansion. Here we are presented with the idea that increase is, first and foremost, indicating dynamic activity. Second, the resultant effect of the activities undertaken is the complete realisation of whatever we achieve. Regarding the idea of expansion as a process, the emphasis indicated here is concerned with "increase, enlargement, or development."[11] However, this expansion does not happen because one wishes it to be so. Only through exerted efforts and spent resources is this made possible. Therefore, the increase anticipated gets achieved when we intentionally and wisely invest time, money, and other resources. To argue that expansion is experienced through great sacrifice is very much in order!

Therefore, expansion as a state of being is the effect of sacrifices made. The extent to which something grows and develops is dependent on the work that one has put in. The symbiotic relationship that labouring and productivity represent is what this aspect of the definition reveals.

---

[10] *Collins English Dictionary*, 569.

[11] Ibid.

Concerning the Ministerial capacity, for example, it encapsulates the following and possibly much more:

- The theological growth achieved through the particular studies one has completed.
- The new skills gained through ministry engagement under the supervision of a more learned, experienced, and mature Minister.
- The extended audience that one now ministers to as a direct result of embarking on new ways of delivering ministry to different communities and neighbourhoods.
- The extent to which, by one's influence, previously hostile and segregated communities, businesses, and companies are far more respectful, engaging, and collaborative.

It may seem that we are overloading the subject of this work by pairing capacity and expansion when capacity is intrinsically dynamic. However, the underlying idea of emphasising the necessity of highlighting capacity's components, as explored earlier, cannot be achieved without the deliberate inclusion of the value which the noun *expansion* carries.

The primary motivation behind this book is to successfully provoke Ministers of grace to become proactive in developing every bestowed ability and the skills that are intrinsic to them, for greater involvement in the service of Jesus's Church, in a world that is yet languishing in darkness and despair. To become mature through the practice of the divinely established spiritual discipline of study and radical obedience under the Holy Spirit's leading and influence is to have a more significant outcome for righteousness and justice where sin and darkness appear to be prevailing. Disabling the devil's reign of terror and bringing the kingdom of God from heaven to earth is the plan that serves as motivation for the production of this book.

In bringing this chapter to a close, there are other vital synonyms of expansion that we would like to highlight and comment on, primarily because of the additional insights they promise to our learning about the subject of capacity expansion. We hope this will help to consolidate all we have previously learned about capacity expansion. We are also encouraged to embrace this valued plan for higher productivity, which this book calls us to consider seriously, amidst the current context of political upheavals and uncertainties that historical situations have engendered.[12] The stark realities of socio-economic dislocation, emotional distress and mental ill-health,[13] and religious pluralism[14] are not just subjects for debates amongst academics and politicians. They are terms used to frame the lived experiences of countless numbers of people across the world. Such harsh and cruel realities along with religious persecution[15] must be faced head-on, even as we grow and develop our capacities in advancing the work of Jesus's Church and that of the kingdom of God here on earth.

1. Growing

Growing is the first of the synonyms of expansion to be explored. *Growing* is a verb that speaks about movement; it is concerned with an "increase in size or development".[16] Increasing in strength, acquiring new properties, and rising in influence and expanding one's reach over a given territory are consistent with the vitality of what it means to grow. Growing is a term that has a broad spectrum. It touches on organic things as well as non-organic ones. Items and creatures possessing a biological system are included in our presentation of organic growth.

In contrast, such things as finance and business are in view when we speak of non-organic growth. Equally, it focuses on the spiritual and the intangible, such as grace, love, faith, and peace. Because growing is implicitly positive, the type of movement identified here is neither frantic nor uncoordinated. Such negativity is not featured because growing is both positive and dynamic. The associated synonyms of growing that we discussed below help us understand the dynamic character of increasing. We must take time to study these synonyms of *increasing*. We stand to gain

---

12   Daron Acemoglu and James A. Robinson, *Why Nations Fail: The Origins of Power, Prosperity and Poverty* (London: Profile, 2012).

13   Dinesh Bhugra, "Migration, Distress and Cultural Identity," *British Medical Bulletin* 69, no. 1 (June 2004, 129–141, https://doi.org/10.1093/bmb/ldh007 (accessed 7 December 2019).

14   Alister E. McGrath, ed., *The Christian Theology Reader, Fifth Edition* (Oxford, Wiley Blackwell, 2017), 506–521.

15   John Foxe, *Foxe's Book of Martyrs* (New Kensington, PA: Whitaker House, 1981).

16   *Collins English Dictionary*, 720.

many insights from the various ways we, as children of God, can grow in the substance of our faith, the components of our ministry, and our influence and effectiveness, even in the ordinary things we do in the world.

We cannot expect to minister to our generation effectively, and to those who will become our future leaders, with the restrictive mode of knowledge acquisition and information-sharing techniques that we have inherited from our predecessors. I am not suggesting that we discount them and deny our antecedents the place of importance they truly deserve in the expansive ministry and witness of the Church of the Lord Jesus Christ in the world. In celebration of our ancestors, those who established the foundation in which our faith now anchors and facilitated our spiritual formation, it is time for this generation to rise and advance the vision for ministerial growth, development, and excellence in service delivery. It is the privilege of those to whom the Holy Spirit's anointing has come to rise to the challenge of leadership and advance the work of Jesus's Church to the next stage of generational transition.

It is not in fear of showing dissent to our predecessors or a callous departure from what they offered that we undertake the vital challenge of growing our capacity. But it is in response to the Holy Spirit's calling and direction that we willingly embrace this challenge. Our predecessors expect us to become richer in knowledge, and more effective in service and spiritual influence than what they accomplished. They expected that we would build on the foundation they left us. Although there is a requirement for us to maintain our precious faith (see fig 2.2), there remains a need to adopt new and creative ways to facilitate knowledge development for capacity expansion, ministry development, and effectiveness in our constant changing contexts of service. To become proactive in a quest of this magnitude is one way in which the current generation of Ministers can bring much joy to the hearts of all concerned. The Lord Jesus Christ expects us to do more significant works than those He achieved through the course of His ministry as the incarnated Word of God (John 14:12). Even so, our predecessors are expecting us to become involved in new and innovative ways of producing empowering spiritual knowledge for faith expansion and excellence in service delivery for Church growth and the glory of God.

Figure 2.2
The Apostles Creed[17]
(Core Beliefs of the Christian's Faith)

I believe in God the Father Almighty,
Maker of heaven and earth;
And in Jesus Christ his only Son our Lord;
who was conceived of the Holy Spirit,
born of the Virgin Mary,
suffered under Pontius pilot,
was crucified, died and buried;
and descended into Hades.
On the third day, He rose again from the dead.
He ascended into heaven,
and is sitting on the right hand of God the Father Almighty.
Whence, he shall come to judge the quick and the dead.
I believe in the Holy Spirit;
the holy catholic church;
the communion of the saints;
the forgiveness of sins;
the resurrection of the body;
and the life everlasting.
Amen.

2. *Developing*

Renowned Guyanese scholar and activist Walter Rodney offers a definition of development in which he suggests that "development in human society is a many-sided process."[18] He argues that "at the level of the individual, it implies increased skills and capacity, greater freedom, creativity, and self-discipline, responsibility and material wellbeing."[19] Rodney's understanding of development carries an inclusivity spectrum that begins with individuals'

---

[17] Stewart Briscoe, *The Apostles' Creed: Beliefs That Matter* (Wheaton IL., Harold Shaw), 1994.

[18] Walter Rodney, *How Europe Underdeveloped Africa* (Abuja: Panaf, 1972), 1.

[19] Ibid., 1.

inner world and then concludes with the dynamic expression of the developed individuality that caters to the welfare and perpetuation of *whole* persons.

Although this definition of development came out of a socio-economic and political context, it appears to capture some essential spiritual virtues that Ministers of Grace would expect to possess knowingly. Although the lens through which Rodney perceived the vital categories of development is primarily socio-political, one would be forgiven to think that they are drawn from biblical theology. Perhaps the presence and influence of religious institutions in Western societies contribute to shaping the developmental categories he advanced. For Rodney, personal development and that of the community within which individuals seek to strive are inseparable. This symbiotic developmental operation appears explicit in the following argument he offered in highlighting the complexities of individuals' development and the restraining power of the socio-political state within which such a project is pursued.

> Some of these are virtually moral categories and are difficult to evaluate-depending as they do on the age in which one lives, one's class origins, and one's special code of what is right and what is wrong. However, what is indisputable is the achievement of any of these aspects of personal achievement is very much tied in with the state of society as a whole.[20]

Personal development and the state of the society in which one lives and operates, appear to be inseparable. The fusion of the dynamic forces of political economy and the unrestraint striving of the individual human spirit exists because the institutions located at the heart of any culture are pertinent to the socialisation of individuals born within it.[21] Therefore, established institutions of society function to influence an individual's identity formation and nurture their development in the world. The legal, political, social, and religious institutions of the community are never passive agencies. They are dynamic agencies by which the powerbrokers in society seek to create and maintain the status quo.

For the disciples of the Lord Jesus Christ to develop the personhood and the identity and capacity intrinsic to them, a unique countercultural

---

[20] Ibid., 1.

[21] Anthony Giddens, *Sociology, Second Edition* (Cambridge: Polity, 2004), 59–88.

societal perspective must be cultivated under the claims of the faith. While evaluating the nature of the development in such a complex societal state, Christian disciples should consciously reject the promoted secular and existential model of society and adhere to a biblical, spiritual one. This radical, Christ-centred call does not in any way negate the vitality of skills and capacity development. Self-discipline, the pursuit of liberty, creative exploration, material well-being, and personal responsibility are vital expressions of our conformity to a Christ-centred way of being. This call to a Christ-centred way of being is one of the objectives of the redemptive mission of Jesus Christ (John 8:31–34, 10:10b). The real and enormous difference that a biblical, spiritual model brings to this evaluation is one of the more substantive and unchanging bases, which occupies an indestructible foundation in the faithful identity of the Sovereign Lord God Jehovah and the inspired Word that He gave for human salvation.

We hold to the view that the Church of the Lord Jesus Christ, with the moral obligations that it places on every person who is an adherent of Jesus and His teachings, constitutes a category of importance against which to evaluate the features of development which Rodney identified at the individual level. Suppose no other community is reasonably equipped to offer a template for assessing the moral categories identified above. In that case, we are confident that the Church of Jesus Christ, with the inspired scriptures and the Holy Spirit, is equipped and appropriately located in the world for such a necessary task.

Increased skills and capacity, the first of the moral categories mentioned by Rodney, is very much tied into the following spiritual directives given to each Minister of grace.

> Therefore, I remind you to stir up the gift of God, which is in you through the laying on of my hands. For God has not given us a spirit of fear, but of power and of love and of a sound mind. (2 Tim. 1:6–7)

> Be diligent to present yourself approved to God, a worker who does not need to be ashamed, rightly dividing the word of truth. (2 Tim. 2:15)

> Grow in grace and knowledge of our Lord and Saviour Jesus Christ. (2 Pet. 3:18)

As it pertains to the capacities bestowed upon believers by the Lord, the theme of growth and development is very much encouraged by Paul and Peter. The language in which Paul and Peter couched their admonition to grow and develop the capabilities which their respective audiences received from the Lord is directive in tone. Therefore, expanding our capacities as Ministers of grace is not optional.

Greater freedom is the second of the moral categories mentioned. It comes about through an increase of knowledge and the understanding it generates. This greater liberty is at the heart of the instruction which the Lord Jesus gave to a group of Jews who were beginning to develop an interest in Him. He states, "If you abide in My Word, you are My disciples indeed. And you shall know the truth and the truth shall make you free" (John 8:31–32). True freedom comes through knowledge rightly understood and faithfully applied. The knowledge that liberates is not the kind that lacks spiritual authenticity. It is the knowledge that has its origins in the works and purpose of God, which depends on the might of the Holy Spirit and is accountable to Him in judgement, that truly liberates. Because Holy Spirit–inspired knowledge is as enduring and credible even as He is in His personhood, identity, and integrity, we stand to benefit ourselves and our community positively when we have surrendered to Him.

Creativity and self-discipline, the third and fourth elements of Rodney's moral categories, are spiritual virtues that the Holy Spirit promotes in Hebrews 4:12 and Galatians 5:23, respectively. It is neither the evil inventions that Paul denounced in Romans 1:30 nor the blinkered self-will of those who make carnal passions the goals of their existence that he later challenged in Galatians 5:19–21 that we are here affirming. Creativity and self-discipline are virtues that enhance the cohesion and longevity of the human community as designed by God. Importantly, this priority objective happens whenever the Word and the Spirit work the will of God in the human soul (Isa. 55:10–11; Eph. 3:20–21).

What can we say about the components of responsibility and material well-being? Are they not the vital truths that are interlinked through the practice of reciprocal service as so carefully outlined in 1 Corinthians 12:4–11 and 1 Peter 4:10–11 by the anointed apostles of the Lord? For communal development, each disciple received an anointing from the Lord. All that the Holy Spirit bestows to believers contributes to the collective expression of the life of which Jesus Christ invested in His Church. This collective expression of unity in worship and service is one such feature that characterises the Church of Jesus Christ. Despite the evident variation and Ministry scopes that are intrinsic to its nature, the Church of Jesus Christ operates in unity by the presence and power of the Holy Spirit. No one is exempt from the service which the Holy Spirit administers in the Church of the Lord Jesus Christ. This Spirit-led service is inclusive. It incorporates each disciple as a valued member within the Body of Christ and lively stones in the eternal edifice for the habitation of God (1 Cor. 12:12–31; 1 Pet. 2:5).

Therefore, development as a synonym of expansion is not just concerned with increasing, although this is one of its prominent features. As indicated in Rodney's definition and further explained in the discussion that ensued, development is about being mature (as shown in the elements of self-discipline) and being responsible. Being able to restrain oneself and effectively manage one's passions are the hallmarks of spiritually maturing people. To possess a fledgling disposition concerning the management of emotions and duty is to be likened to children who are emotionally and mentally underdeveloped. To be immature in spiritual things is to be "tossed to and fro and carried about with every wind of doctrine, by the trickery of men, in the cunning craftiness of deceitful plotting" (Eph. 4:14).

Therefore, development for the people of God means many things. It is inclusive of being confident in the identity we each possess by grace in Christ through the indwelling presence and mighty workings of the Holy Spirit, as well as having an increased awareness and understanding of the capacity we received from God in grace through faith in Christ Jesus. This development is about being able to confidently give a reasonable response to anyone who asks about the hope we have in Jesus, and also that of being in a position to employ our gifts competently to others for the glory of God (1 Pet. 3:15, 4:7–11).

3. Increasing

One of the other synonyms of *expansion* is *increase*. The concept of increase has to do with growth or maximisation. To apply the idea of inflation to the five essential characteristics of capacity is to paint a picture of inspiration. This picture serves the purpose of motivating Ministers to become more engaged in positive actions that lead to personal maturity and effectiveness in Holy Spirit-directed service. Because we are each allowed the abilities and power which the Lord bestowed to increase through time spent in the Word (Ps. 1:1–6), in prayer for others (John 15:8–9) and service to them (Matt. 25:20–23), growth should not be an exception but the evident trait that marks the Christian life. By practising the spiritual disciplines of reading, praying, and serving, our capacity for more of that which is available from the storehouse of the Lord, should be increased. Practising these spiritual disciplines should, in turn, produce an increase in our godly influence and service effectiveness amongst communities and over regions in a way that demonstrates the facilitation of the missional plan, which situates at the centre of the vision to which we give ourselves resolutely and in undeterred commitment.

The passion that lies at the heart of the increase in this book promotes the vitality of God's kingdom in various observable features such as mercy, righteousness, and justice. It was for advancing these spiritual virtues that God established Abraham and his descendants in the earth (Gen. 18:17–19). In developing this plan to its complete substantive realisation, the Spirit of the Sovereign Lord spoke through the prophet Isaiah, foretelling the work of God's Messiah, which gives credence to the spiritual authenticity of the eternal nature of its vital features of mercy, righteousness, and justice. It is within the contents of the following prophetic declarations that we are to find these critical features of the redemptive purpose of the Lord's Messiah.

> For unto us a Child is born, unto us a Son is given; And the government will be upon His shoulder. And His name will be called Wonderful, Counsellor, Mighty God, Everlasting Father, Prince of Peace. Of the increase of *His* government and peace *there will be* no end, Upon the throne of David and over His kingdom, to order it and establish it with judgment and justice from that time forward, even forever. The zeal of the LORD of hosts will perform this. (Isa. 9:6–7)

> The voice of one crying in the wilderness: "Prepare the way of the Lord; make straight in the desert a highway for our God. Every valley shall be exalted, and every mountain and hill brought low; the crooked places shall be made straight and rough places smooth; the glory of the Lord shall be revealed, and all flesh shall see it together; for the mouth of the Lord has spoken it. (Isa. 40:3–5)

The missional agenda to which Jesus gave Himself is the very one to which He has called all who are members of His Church. He promised that our involvement in service with Him would result in increased effectiveness and productivity (John 14:12–14). Increase in capacity for those at the forefront of the work of Jesus's Church is not concerned with personal fame or ego pampering—no, not in the least! An increase in ability, power, understanding, intellectual capability, and productive output has only one desire at heart: the manifestation of the kingdom of God in substantive, measurable features of mercy, righteousness, and justice. These constitute the method of accountability that God shall use in judging the nations. By them, some will secure admission to the kingdom which the Father prepared from the foundation of the world, while others will share the lake of fire prepared for the devil and his angels (Matt. 25:31–46).

4. Changing: A Feature of Capacity Expansion

As a feature of capacity expansion, change focuses attention on several factors that are pertinent to Ministers' mental disposition and their actual participation in the delivery of those responsibilities that are intrinsic to the role in which they function. It is not so much change in the physical context or location from where Ministers serve that is of primary concern here, although this has an essential bearing on who and what Ministers are. Contextual change can affect the emotional and mental state of the people who happen to be at the centre of such realities. Exodus 32 and Psalm 137 provide two examples in which contextual variations effected significant change in the emotional and mental state of the people of Israel. In the former, Israel reverts to the vain religious practices they observed in Egypt, all because they resented the fact that their leader Moses was absent from them for about forty days. Their cry for Egypt was the surface reason given for their outrageous behaviour. However, the deeper reason for such a rebellion was their inability to discern what it meant to be in a covenant relationship with God.

Similarly, the latter passage offers further evidence of the same group of people (different generations but descendants of Abraham, Isaac, and Israel) exhibiting signs of change in their emotional and mental state even as they were driven as slaves from Jerusalem to Babylon. Contrastingly, we have people such as Joshua, Caleb, and Daniel and his friends who happened to have been in similar contexts as those on which we have already commented. Unlike the majority, these latter heroes retained a positive emotional and mental state, although they were in captivity. They lived and served the purpose of God's kingdom in the resolved emotional and spiritual state they cultivated within their previous habitat; see Numbers 14 and Daniel 1–3 for the substance of the stories. However, it is the change that is central to the development of personal beliefs and the Minister's emotional and mental attitude that is being promoted here for examination. So, what kind of acquired skills or character disposition are required for withstanding the imposing forces that contextual change generates for Ministers of God?

We are aware that change at any level of human experience can be challenging—even those changes that appear to offer fortune. Moving from one employer to another, changing from a single person status to that of a married person, and living with a disability caused by accident come with their particular set of challenges. With each of these changes, experiences come with varying degrees of stress for all concerned. Other situations that produce unimaginable stress include becoming a parent, migrating from one country to another, and having to say goodbye to a loved one because of various circumstances such as divorce or death. These are some of the actual changes that are experienced by people throughout the world. Christians do not escape such realities. All these possible changing situations come with varying degrees of difficulties that can affect those who experience them. For some, the loss of self and identity are the results of the change experience they encounter. Still, for others the situations experienced have propelled them to heights and locations in the social strata never before imagined. The most significant factors that have determined these varied outcomes for those subjected to life's challenges are the possession, or lack thereof, of the essential resources of resilience, perseverance, hope, emotional stamina, and social awareness.

The experience of suicide has become prominent amongst young people and young adults in the United Kingdom and other parts of the world.[22] This increase comes about because many who have attempted ending their lives have not cultivated the necessary resources required

---

22   Murad M. Khan, "Suicide Prevention and Developing Countries," *Journal of the Royal Society of Medicine* 98,, no. 10 (2005), 459–463, https://doi.org/10.1258/jrsm.98.10.459.

to navigate the change-oriented experiences they encounter.[23] The act of suicide may also result from the change that has occurred within the minds and the emotions of those who attempt to and those who succeed in ending their lives.[24] From this complex web of human feelings and reasonings, we observe a series of changes happening at different levels of personalities, whenever challenging situations and traumatic life experiences occur.

Interestingly, we do not always discern the actual nature and specific occasions when internal changes occur, unless those who have such experiences, disclose. However, we know about those physical changes primarily because they are the results, impacts, or effects of the generally undiscerned mental and emotional changes that usually happen at the personality's internal level and are therefore concealed. It is at the physical (i.e., carnal) level that we become aware of the presence of difficulty. Excessive alcohol consumption, isolating oneself from the company one generally enjoyed, excessive indulgence in physical activities, unusually aggressive behaviour, self-harming, refusal of food, and attempted suicide are the manifested symptoms of emotional and mental fatigue and trauma.

Not everyone who has encountered challenging situations undergoes changes that are detrimental to one's life and existence on earth. Other people have somehow managed to access vital resources, even amidst the difficulties encountered, and have succeeded in embarking on a successful and prosperous path. Dave Pelzer's books *A Child Called "It"*[25] and *The Lost Boy*[26] provide an excellent example of how personal resilience and hope provided a pathway out of what appeared to have been an extraordinarily dismal and despairing situation.

In person-centred counselling, change is perceived as necessary for personal development but is sometimes difficult to attain. This is primarily the case because of the nature of the process that individuals must negotiate to experience the change desired. In certain instances, the possible impact

---

[23] Richard L. Gregory, ed., *The Oxford Companion to the Mind* (Oxford: Oxford University Press, 1987), 759.

[24] S. Abrutyn and S. A. Mueller, "Toward a Cultural-Structural Theory of Suicide: Examining Excessive Regulation and Its Discontents," *Sociological Theory* 36, no. 1 (2018), 48–66, https://doi.org/10.1177/0735275118759150.

[25] Dave Pelzer, *A Child Called "It"* (London: Orion, 1995).

[26] Dave Pelzer, *The Lost Boy* (London: Orion, 1997).

that persons seeking change are required to embrace can also serve to prevent desired change from occurring.[27] For example, persons from some cultural backgrounds conceal the decision they make to become disciples of the Lord Jesus Christ because of the persecution and possible execution they would suffer should their decision become public.

For the person who engages in the service of Jesus's Church, there is an expectation that positive change will occur in the faith they possess. This change should facilitate growth in the genuine belief that the believer exercises in living and serving. As presented here, change is not suggesting replacing faith with non-faith or some other non-effective spirituality that is contrary and alien to God's Word. We advocate the extent of the development and growth of biblical spiritual faith from "mustard-seed faith" (Luke 17:6) to "great faith" (Matt. 8:10). Therefore, what we promote are the necessary underpinning divine revelations, contained in theological doctrines, which constitute the dynamo that fuels the belief it generates in the heart of the person who receives it in the completeness of its integrity (Rom. 10:9–13). This faith informs the type of attitude that one brings to their living and service experience in the present world. In this regard, change for Christian Ministers is therefore not one-dimensional but multidimensional and very much interconnected.

This is one of the important lessons that Christian Ministers need to grasp if personal, lived experiences and the challenges encountered in the Ministry are to be successfully navigated and managed. Seeing change as multidimensional is vital if bestowed capacity is to undergo growth and development. Viewing the challenges that are invariably encountered as negative situations that believers should detest is not developmental and should not become an established pattern in the lives of Christian Ministers. Spiritual leaders should always keep in mind that God cultivates sturdy and godly character within the valleys of life. Therefore, the heat of the furnace does not destroy the gold but the impurity that it contains (1 Pet. 1:6–9).

To effect change in others by your conformity to God's Word is one aspect of transformation that Christian Ministers should view as positively affecting capacity expansion and development. Being aware of how God's Word affects change in people who receive the ministry delivered by spiritual leaders is essential in capacity expansion and development. It is to this

---

27 Janet Tolan with Rose Cameron, *Skills in Person-Centred Counselling and Psychotherapy, Third Edition* (Los Angeles: Sage, 2017), 6–8.

positive cause and effect paradigm that appointed spiritual leaders should conform. Verified experiences of change in others, resulting from one's life and ministry, provide opportunities for expansion and development in personal faith and ministry practice. Therefore, it is prudent that all concerned are alerted to their occurrence and how we appraise them to ensure that nothing of value escapes or gets robbed from us.

5. Abraham's Story: A Case Study of Change as a Feature of Capacity Expansion

The story of Abraham presents an invaluable case study from which we can learn about some of the possible changes that may occur in a life that is called from the world and offered the opportunity to become God's fellow labourer. From the biblical narrative concerning Abraham, we identify a geographical change from Ur of the Chaldees to the Land of Canaan, and a change in his name from Abram to Abraham. Although these changes were significant in his life, primarily because they were in themselves examples of God's manifested power, it is at the deeper level of his mentality and character that we see more impressive and significant transitions and transformations.

Throughout his journey from Ur of the Chaldees to the Land of Canaan, Abraham's growth in faith and the attitude he adopted before the Lord is a physical description of his spiritual transformation from being a worshipper of idols to becoming a man of faith and God's friend. Electing to accept God's revealed plan for his life, and God's process and methods in bringing to substantive realisation all the promises associated with it, is a most compelling example of faith that all believers should highly regard. The outward and other-focused mentality which replaced the obsessive and insular attitude he demonstrated concerning the heir he desired, in addition to those vital elements identified earlier, constitute an example of the multidimensional change we are here advocating for as a feature of capacity expansion. We assert that capacity increase engenders change at the various spiritual, social, intellectual, and operational levels of the believer.

The narrative of Genesis 12–18 provides extensive details of a twenty-four-year transformational process to which the Lord subjected Abraham. This process accounted for a series of developmental experiences that brought about his holistic transformation, which resulted in the expansion of his faith capacity and the subsequent positive attitude he adopted and demonstrated before the Lord's presence towards the inhabitants of Sodom and Gomorrah. Some of the essential features of this process of change are summarised in the change model illustration below in figure 2.3. It is important to note how each episode of divine encounter that Abram experienced served as a vital feature of the change process to which God subjected him.

We organised the model in a grid format for easy reference. This model allows the learner to identify some of the divine encounters Abraham experienced in his journey with God. This grid contains the revelations Abraham received about his new life during his encounter experiences with the Lord. The grid also includes suggestions about the type of change that occurred in his mind towards the Lord, about himself, the circumstances he experienced, and the people he met throughout the process of his journey. Situated at the heart of this change process for Abraham is the relationship which the Lord called Abraham to enjoy with Him. This relationship provided the real context within which he experienced the various changes accounted for in the narrative of Abraham's story. All that the Lord demanded of him became possible not because Abraham had perfect faith from the beginning but because of the grace that the facilitating presence of the Lord afforded him.

Realising that God takes full responsibility for determining the contexts within which He facilitates the holistic transformation of His chosen servants should provide courage for us to submit to His will and purpose (Deut. 8:1–5). The value of this truth is of critical importance for God's servants. It prevents unnecessary worrying and serves to bolster the divinely desired disposition of authentic spiritual rest and devotional obedience to God's commands (Ps. 23:1–6; Rom. 8:28–29).

Job realised this truth at a very turbulent time in his life. He eventually arrived at the place of submission to God's will and purpose after navigating the prolonged period of counselling to which his wife and friends subjected him (Job 2:9–10, and chapters 4, 5, 8, 11, 15, 18, 20, and 22). Finally, he confined himself to trusting the Lord instead of spending his time worrying about things he could not alter (Job 42: 1–6). The apostle Paul discovered the value of this truth in his faith journey at a time when he desired deliverance from what he considered to be an ordeal that threatened his relationship with God. But the answer he received from the Lord, after spending time in supplication, granted much-needed assurance and courage to submit to the experience from which he wanted the Lord to deliver him. He wanted deliverance from what he termed "a thorn in the flesh", but God wanted absolute submission so that He could perfectly manifest His grace and strength in him (2 Cor. 12:7–10).

The Lord's presence is the natural means by which the change He demands of those He calls into intimacy with Himself is achieved. Relationship with the Lord God does not seek to diminish the potency of the purpose to which He calls a man or a woman. On the contrary, it aims to improve and expand, refine and empower—and not just the vision but the person. This facilitates the expansion of the vitality which He bestows at conversion—a vitality destined to progress through the Lord's activity of redemption! Importantly, this way of becoming God's faithful friend is not restricted to Abraham or confined to the pages of history; it is the normal path for all who positively respond to the appeal of the Spirit and the call of God. Time invested in exploring Abraham's life, and the relationship he shared with the Lord, will yield invaluable insights. It offers suggestions concerning how we might begin to evaluate the responses we have given to the Spirit of God, concerning the various situations in which He placed us for the growth and development of the capacity we received from Him.

Figure 2.3
Change: A Feature of Capacity Expansion and Development
The Abrahamic Change Model

No.	Information/ Revelation	Type and Nature of Change Intended	Dispositional Attitude	Reference	Patterns for Adoption
1.	Initial revelation: A call to geographical, relational, parental, personal, and status transformation	Mental and emotional changes concerning personal private desire: Such changes were to be facilitated by the revelation God gave concerning His identity and the power by which He would bring to realisation the promises He made	A response of obedience that is marked by sacrificing established emotional ties	Gen. 12:1–3	Complete submission to the transformational process that is intrinsic to the call of God and is necessary for the substance of the call to be realised.

No.	Information/ Revelation	Type and Nature of Change Intended	Dispositional Attitude	Reference	Patterns for Adoption
2.	Additional revelation: Affirming the initial promise concerning his parental status, and another pledge of earthly possession	Greater mental clarity concerning his parental status, which facilitated and increased his faith in the Lord God	A response in worship manifested in the building of altars in the name of the Lord	Gen. 12:4–9	A worshipful disposition is an invaluable quality which demonstrates our submission to God and the purpose He reveals for our lives.
3.	Additional revelation: Experiencing the providential care and protection of the Lord during horrid times and in a strange land	Acquiring valuable insights about the faithfulness of God to protect and preserve by His promises, thus, enabling growth in faith	Humility manifested in a trusting response to all that God commands	Gen. 12:10–20	We must seek to develop a humble, trusting relationship with God, wherein our dependence on Him is such as a child upon their parents.
4.	Additional revelation, which focused on the extent of his parental heritage within an inherited land	Increased information about the promised blessing presented in a vision within the context of a geographical expanse for faith development	The response of obedience in exploration and worship, as represented in the building of an altar	Gen.13:1–19	Erecting monuments to commemorate significant milestones in one's journey with the Lord is vital to personal faith development.
5.	Affirming the mission of rescuing captives through the ministry of the priest, thus providing insight into his role as dispenser of divine justice within a world where "to sin" comes naturally	Affording additional evidence of divine protection: this served as the means for increasing faith in God	A response in worship commemorated by giving of a tithe	Gen. 14:1–24	Tithing to the Lord's Priest is an expression of confident appreciation for the inexhaustible source one has in the Lord.

No.	Information/ Revelation	Type and Nature of Change Intended	Dispositional Attitude	Reference	Patterns for Adoption
6.	Additional revelation: Reaffirming precious promises, correcting the human propensity to fear and igniting the fire of faith in his mind and soul for a future that cannot fade away	Affording clarity in perception and thought concerning the immutable character of the Lord, which served to consolidate faith and instil hope in a future with God that will never fade away	Adopting an attitude of faith towards the Lord and all that He promised, which allows for a deeper relationship – resulting in increased or further revelations	Gen 15:1–21	Fears and frustrations are to be reported to the Lord and not to be concealed and merely pondered.
7.	Self-help plan: Making choices and decisions based solely on human reasoning and misinterpretation of the timing and method by which the Lord proposes to bring to realisation what He has promised!	Reverting to natural human reasoning and carnal behaviour: mental and spiritual regression	Rebellion necessitated by ignorance and a felt need for a male child; a false premise of peace	Gen. 16:1–16	Devising self-help strategies to bring into being God's promises is never acceptable.
8.	Additional revelation: Final lessons in preparation for divine service— the Lord's timing is not determined by human ability or nature. The Lord is not fearful of old age and barrenness!	The Lord requires total sanctification; He will not change His plan to meet carnal desires; covenant communion is needed, and this demands the complete mind, spirit, and body of the one called by the Lord	An attitude of submission necessitating holistic transformation in readiness for the miracle of the Lord	Gen. 17:1–27	Submission to the will of God is a requirement that is not seasonal but one that encompasses the entirety of one's life.

No.	Information/ Revelation	Type and Nature of Change Intended	Dispositional Attitude	Reference	Patterns for Adoption
9.	Fuller revelation: The Lord manifested Himself, clothed in human flesh	The realisation of the power of authentic faith, emotional and mental peace, confidence to engage in intercession, other-focused mentality	Other-focused mentality refocuses the spotlight from self to others!	Gen. 18:1–33	Realising one's role in serving the welfare of others keeps one focused on the real redemptive mission of God.
10.	A critical lesson in spiritual operations: The promise and accomplishments of the Lord take precedence over the works of the flesh and carnal ambition.	Faith efficacy revealed: The manifested product of carnal desires must be rejected for the effect of faith to thrive without hindrance	Cultivating a character that depends on faith's reasoning instead of being directed by emotions and sentiment, however dear they may be	Gen. 21:1–19	Carnal acquisitions must be sacrificed to allow that which is spiritual to thrive and come to maturity.
11.	Revelation on human relationship: Managing neighbourly affairs and relationships in a way that demonstrates the holy integrity one possesses in transformational covenant relationship with the Lord	Regarding and treating others in accordance with the standard that personal relationship with the Lord dictates	Being fair in one's dealings with others	Gen. 21:22–34	Be equitable in one's dealings with others.

No.	Information/ Revelation	Type and Nature of Change Intended	Dispositional Attitude	Reference	Patterns for Adoption
12.	Important revelation concerning the perfecting of faith in the furnace of trials: The believer's life should be bound entirely with the Lord and not so much in the gifts He bestows	The absolute surrendering of all that one possesses in personhood and property to the Lord; radical, holistic transformation	Living in utter dependence on the LORD's utterances	Gen. 22:1–19	Be prepared for the acid test of your faith.

We hope your sense of appreciation for spiritual processing is heightened upon realising the type of journey Abraham went through to become established in the earth as the archetype of spiritual sanctification and divine empowerment. From being an idol worshiper in Ur of the Chaldees to becoming God's friend and the possessor of the land that God promised accounts for a process designed and administrated by Jehovah God. This journey was marked by all sorts of challenges and the vital changes that facilitated the holistic transformation from Abram to Abraham! These changes were not just related to physical locations; they were deeply mental, emotional, and spiritual. To say that the journey, and the various processes which characterised it, did a number on Abraham that left him wholly transformed would most definitely be an understatement! In fact, the man, Abraham, was deconstructed and then reconstructed by God throughout the twenty-six years of history that we have sketched in the change model grid. God knew the type of partner He wanted Abraham to become and used various circumstances and people to bring him to that standard. Through such changes, he grew in knowledge, understanding, and the unfeigned wisdom that allowed him to become the power-packed man we have come to know and celebrate. His capacity for friendship with God—required to parent the promised son, and needed for making intercession for nations—grew and matured through an extensive and adventurous process that had personal and community transformation as the end product.

Therefore, capacity expansion is much more than acquiring additional technical knowledge that enables those who serve in the Church of the Lord Jesus Christ to offer better presentations of the gospel message to those comprising their targeted audience. By this inference, we are in no way denouncing technical knowledge or wanting to minimise its intrinsic value in the various ministries of the Church. Preaching, teaching, and counselling are prominent areas of ministry requiring specialised knowledge. This is an aspect of the Minister's capacity that should experience expansion and development, as it constitutes a standardised feature of divinely bestowed capacity. Technical knowledge should develop alongside other essential aspects of a Minister's capacity.

For example, the faith underlying the work Ministers deliver in ministry, a positive attitude towards the work that the Holy Spirit schedules to be accomplished, and loving the people comprising their targeted audience constitute vital features of an increased capacity worth recognising and celebrating. As represented in the various modes of change that marked the process of Abraham's transformation, becoming the person who wins the favour and confidence of the Lord and being established by Him as an icon of divine faith is invaluable to capacity growth and development. A representation of audacious hope and a model of sincere love in a dark and wicked world which God targets for redemption are the very goals that our journey with the Lord intends to achieve.

We hope those involved in the service of Jesus's Church carries a desire for the capacity they possess to expand and develop. The process of transformation to which God subjects His chosen servants provides a context to evaluate how desired capacity expansion and development are produced in us, not just at a superficial level but at the core of our being. There must be internal changes if external changes are to be experienced and regarded as sacred and honourable. Suppose the critical inner transformation is not achieved? In that case, any increase in knowledge or wealth will lead to pride, the exploitation of others, and one's eventual demise. To be God's friend is to be located in a substantive relationship for all times and seasons. The life of Abraham depicts this. Let us now realise that it is to a change process, not dissimilar to what Abraham was subjected to, that the Lord has called us. We can become much more than what we currently are if we are prepared to embrace all that the Sovereign Lord has called us to take unto ourselves. Abraham's life is not just a story located in history; it is a pattern given, to which we are to conform, for impactful living and service, and the ultimate glory of God.

4. An Evaluation of Personal Learning

Choose one of the various aspects of development presented earlier and briefly reflect on its relevance as a means for expanding an aspect of your ministry capacity.

CHAPTER 3

Biblical Theology, Capacity Expansion, and Development

But grow in the grace and knowledge of our Lord and Saviour
Jesus Christ. (2 Peter 3:18)

Introduction

There is no better place from which we should seek understanding
regarding matters of critical importance concerning the capacity we possess
and how we can grow and develop it for adequate service, besides availing
ourselves to the counsel of the Inspired Word of God. The "Scripture[s]
[are] given by inspiration of God, and is profitable for doctrine, for reproof,
for correction, for instruction in righteousness, that the man [woman] of
God may be complete, thoroughly equipped for every good work" (2 Tim.
3:16–17). This fact makes them an indispensable source from which we
can learn about capacity expansion and development.

We will restrict our discussion scope on the above subject to four critical
areas for this work. First, we will explore the idea of capacity expansion
as a feature of the grace which God has lavished upon humankind by
focusing attention on Genesis 1:26-28 and Luke 2:52. Second, we will
explore the theme of capacity expansion and development in the teachings
of Jesus. Paul's and Peter's treatment of the subject of capacity expansion

and development amongst the people of God will be the third and fourth sets of teachings explored, respectively.

1. Capacity Expansion as a Feature of God's Bestowed Grace

- **Genesis 1:26–28**

Capacity building is one of the first significant lessons presented to us in scripture concerning God's dealings with the people He created for His pleasure and glory (Rev. 4:11). Genesis 1:26–27 reveals God's intention concerning the creation of humankind and the actual realisation of that intention in substantive form. God created humans, male and female, in His image and according to His likeness. The verse which immediately follows reveals the most dynamic truth that directly addresses the heart of the subject under exploration. This verse opens with a wonderful and positive statement: "And God blessed them." One would believe that God had accomplished what He announced He would do at the point when He created humankind: to accept that the man and the woman, whom God created, were fully competent for the specific purposes for which He created them. "And God blessed them" appears to offer something additional. It suggests that God added something to those He made to procreate and replenish the earth and exercise dominion over all that exists on the planet. Whatever God added to the human beings He created is understood and confined to the term He used to describe the very act and the substance of that which He bestowed. The term used is *blessed*.

Blessed is an English word translated from the Hebrew word *barak*, which means "to kneel: by implication to bless God (as an act of adoration), or (vice-versa) man (as a benefit)".[28] Although some essential synonyms such as *holy, sacred, sanctified,* and *consecrated* are paired with *blessed*, it is not just the disposition or status of the object receiving the Lord's bestowed grace that we are here seeking to promote. The fact of divine empowerment for accomplishing feats more remarkable than those we or others may have predicted as expected outcomes in our living and servicing is very much

---

[28] James Strong, *Strong's Exhaustive Concordance of the Bible* (Nashville: Holman Bible Publishers, 1992), 130; *Hebrew and Chaldee Dictionary*, ref. 1288, p. 25.

the point of importance that we hope to communicate and that you fully grasp.

From the content of Genesis 1:28, and the substance of the earlier definition, we can surmise that the very act of God, whereby He blessed the male and the female that He created in His image and likeness, was that of benefiting them with a resource taken from His eternal bounty. Because the current context of exploration concerns humankind and not God, and because the recipient of the good bestowed through the usage of the term *blessed*, we must confine our discussion at this juncture to what God gave humankind at the point of their creation. The act of blessing, which God has undertaken toward the man and the woman whom He created, informs an understanding of the idea of capacity increase.

We hasten to note that the man and woman God created were not unfinished, inferior, or lacking in any way. They were very much like God in the way that God intended that they should be. This position is the only conclusion we can arrive at whenever we consider God's intrinsic holiness and faithfulness. God (Elohim)[29] decided to create "man" (male and female) in His image. Verse 27 of Genesis 1 leaves us without doubt or suspicion that God achieved what He willed. However, verse 28 indicated that God carried out additional work which positively impacted those He created. The narrative states that God chose to bless the people whom He created in His image and likeness.

The activity of blessing is adding vital resources to someone's life. It is concerned with capacity maximisation and increased productivity. Being blessed points to other forms of opportunity through which intrinsic values and potentials become more significant in themselves and in their capability to effect greater productivity.

We are not in the least concerned with the enriching value of the idea that God gave something special, in addition to what He presented at the point of creation, to the man and the woman who bore His image. Realising that God's habit is to bestow in abundance all that He gives in love to the people He created for His pleasure and glory, provides an adequate basis for accepting this revelation. This attitude of divine generosity is evident from the following passages of scripture, which contain the actual language

---

[29] Tim Chester, *Delighting in the Trinity: Why Father, Son and Spirit Are Good News* (The Good Book Company, 2005), 41–42.

that the Spirit inspired holy men to record to articulate the extravagance in which God blesses His people: 1 Samuel 1:9–18, 2:18–21; Romans 8:37–39; Ephesians 3:20–21.

The first two passages (1 Sam. 1:9–18, 2:18–21) offer vital insights concerning the superfluous and extravagant ways in which the Lord God blesses those whom He favours. Hannah desired just one son for the dual purpose of removing her shame and providing a man to be trained to give devotional attendance to the Lord's mission during a period of national spiritual degradation. God answered her prayer most extraordinarily. He blessed her with six children, four sons and two daughters. The third highlighted text (Rom. 8:37–39) offers additional testimony of the Lord's generosity, extravagantly delivered, to those in whose lives His love resides. It speaks to the fact that believers are empowered by God through love in Jesus Christ to extravagantly triumph over every natural and spiritual situation and entity that constitutes a stumbling block, challenging the everlasting relationship that He has called believers to enjoy with Him. In the latter scripture (Eph. 3:20–21), we have evidence of God promising believers more than what they asked for in prayer. It is by the mighty power of God, which is already at work in the lives of believers, that He promises to achieve such an incredible feat.

The Lord's generosity towards those whom He favours is not only found in the scripture passages identified earlier. It is announced in such an elaborate manner throughout the Scriptures that to ignore it or to seek to downplay its importance as a blessing that the Lord bestows to whomsoever He wills, is not only an indication of spiritual blindness but a sin that should be repented of without hesitation or delay.

From the earliest period of human existence, we observe that God announced His intention of ensuring the increase of our capacity by His willingness to add His favour to our lives. He has not created us and left us to just get on with whatever He created us to do. He gives us more by adding to whatever He gave previously so that our capacity can increase to achieve more for the glory of His name. Expanding the capacity that we currently have appears to be an activity that God chooses to do in our lives. Perhaps our response to such a revelation might not be a celebratory dance but a commitment to seeking a greater understanding of what has been bestowed upon us, so that we may grow and expand in discipleship and ministry for God's ultimate glory. The intention to increase the capacity of the people He created and redeemed for the grand purpose of proclaiming His praises (1 Pet. 2:9; Rev. 4:11) is well attested in the Holy Scriptures. We will identify and comment on some of these before bringing this chapter to a close. However, first we invite the reader to take some time to reflect on the material covered so far.

Personal Assessment Tool
What insights have you gained from the exploration of God's act of blessing the man and the woman whom He created, according to Genesis 1:26–28, that you can use to inform your attitude and desire for capacity expansion and development as a child of God and a Minister of grace?

- **Luke 2:52**

It is remarkable that Luke, the evangelist, wrote about the growth and development of Jesus in such human terms (Luke 2:39–40, 52). This revelation takes away some of the mystery surrounding Jesus's identity as a man. It presents His life as a template for inspiring holy ambition and the spiritual discipline of studying the Word of God as a devotional duty for all believers, particularly those who announce that they are leaders in the body of Christ. Engaging with others about the meanings of such an important revelation and the place of priority it deserves in the lives of all who are in covenant with God is intrinsic to our quest for understanding what is presented to us in the scriptures about capacity expansion (Luke 2:41–49; John 15:9–10). There is no ambiguity in the information Luke gave about Jesus growing in His capacity for service as the Lord's appointed Messiah.

These key passages in Luke's gospel offer us essential revelation about the humanity of Jesus. They also point us to what is possible whenever we discipline ourselves by setting time aside to engage with the Word of God. The discipline of studying the Word of God puts us in a position to share the same with others in conversation, concerning its claims and the demands it makes for our meaningful engagement in the life of the Kingdom of God right here on earth.

Concerning the incremental growth and development of Jesus, and with specific regard for the capacity He received from God the Father, Christopher J. H. Wright's scholarly work *Knowing Jesus through the Old Testament* offers many valuable insights. Principally, Wright argues that Jesus studied the Old Testament scriptures and learned about Himself and the work that He was born to fulfil on the earth for the salvation of humanity and the glory of God. Wright states,

> So then, in his humanity as a growing young man and at the point when he entered his public ministry, who did Jesus think he was? What did he think he was destined by God to do? The answer came from his Bible, the Hebrews Scriptures. Jesus would have studied them very thoroughly as a Jewish boy of his generation. He would have learnt large sections by heart, as the rest did. And in those Scriptures Jesus found a rich tapestry of figures, historical persons, sequences of historical events, prophetic pictures and symbols. And in this tapestry, where others saw only a fragmented collection of various figures and hopes, Jesus saw his own face. His Scriptures provided the shape of his identity.[30]

Wright is in no way minimising the vitality of the divinity of Jesus Christ by the critical point he made about the developmental process to which Jesus was subjected as a man. He is pointing us to the truth of the humanity of Jesus and the excellent example He presents to humankind, especially those who believe in God through Him. It is for our learning that Jesus is presented to as a man who grew in wisdom and stature through the discipline of study and service. We would urge that every temptation to dismiss this reason and the insight it provides concerning

---

[30] Christopher J. H. Wright, *Knowing Jesus through the Old Testament, Second Edition* (Downers Grove IL., IVP Academic, 2014), 115.

capacity growth and development, as exemplified by the man Jesus, be resisted forthwith and that you keep all portals to spiritual revelation open. Any attempt to discount the value of the humanity of Jesus and the manner of His human development and expression, in the entire scheme of His life on earth, sabotages an essential part of the redemption plan for fallen humankind. As man, Jesus lived under the gaze of all humanity and in full resistance against the power of sin and the works of the devil, to offer hope to all people about the process by which we grow in grace and favour before the presence of God and our fellow human beings.

As Luke stated, Jesus's development and learning did not all come at once, but gradually. He built His capacity through disciplined study and interaction with others over time. The text is quite clear about its subject and intention. Jesus grew in wisdom and stature and in favour with God the Father and the people who knew Him. He increased in wisdom. His deportment and conversation were of the sort that attracted and held the attention of those who knew Him most favourably.

However, we can understand the potential challenge that some may face in interpreting this particular verse, when, elsewhere in scripture, we are told many beautiful things about the divine nature of Jesus. If Jesus is indeed the Living Incarnate Word of God, as announced by John 1:1–3 and Paul in Philippians 2:5–11, what need would He have to grow in wisdom and stature? Is divinity developmental in its nature? Was Jesus's knowledge of God the Father acquired through incremental processes? In answering these critical questions about Luke 2:52, we advocate that Jesus must be seen as the Holy Spirit reveals Him in the text. He is revealed as a human being, a child born of a woman and fully human, one who engaged in the normal and natural process of human maturation, with its varying incremental growth and development markers. The passage is not focusing on the divinity of Jesus, but on His humanity—the Living Word in human flesh (John 1:14); the Living Word incarnate; the very one who was born to die for the sins of the world (John 1:29; Gal. 4:4).

Without controversy, we assert that as God, Jesus possesses all things consistent with divinity and is therefore not in need of anything. His high-priestly prayer, recorded in John 17:1–5, indicates that he existed with the Father as an equal within the Godhead before His incarnation. There is no evidence of deficit indicated in His pre-incarnate personhood. As God,

He is the same yesterday, today, and forever (Heb. 13:8). His divinity, His constancy as God, which the Holy Spirit intentionally presented in John 1:1–2, is further echoed in Hebrews 13:8. This vital message is concerned with the pre-incarnate Jesus, the Jesus who is the embodiment of the Living Word. Other necessary explorations concerning the two natures of Jesus, and the particular way these interact, will offer invaluable insights beyond the scope of this work. Mark Jones' *A Christian's Pocket Guide to Jesus Christ: An Introduction to Christology*[31] might prove useful as a preparatory read for a more in-depth exploration.

However, as the Living Word incarnate—that is, the Word becoming flesh, which is to say, God becoming a human person by taking on human flesh (John 1:14)—the process of human maturation is therefore applicable. By this, we mean that Jesus, who is the Living Word (Eternal God) incarnated (became a man), was subjected to the very process of development to which all other humans are subjected. This is the very fact—the growth and development of Jesus, the human person—that Luke 2:52 endeavours to promote.

What, then, is the message that we are to be concerned with at this point? This one thing: that the man Jesus modelled capacity expansion, which each believer should fully pursue, especially those fulfilling leadership within the Church. As "the Son of David" (Matt. 1:1; Mark 10:47; Luke 1:30–32), Jesus saw it fit to equip Himself with the fullness of all that God's servants recorded in the law and the prophets so that He was in a position to know and fulfil the purpose for which He was born, as a man in the earth (Matt. 5:17–18; John 17:1–5). Should we, who are called to pattern His examples, expect to follow a different process?

2. Jesus Teaches Believers about Capacity Expansion and Development

Expansion, growth, development, and maturity are very much part and parcel of the work which Jesus came from heaven to accomplish. His presence on earth concerned the kingdom of God and its expansion and

---

[31] Mark Jones, *A Christian's Pocket Guide to Jesus Christ: An Introduction to Christology* (Scotland: Christian Focus, 2012).

influence for the regulation of every affair on earth. John declared that Jesus's coming to the world had to do with the manifestation of God the Father in grace, truth, and glory (John 1:14–18). These vital manifestations of the identity and personhood of God the Father, which are seen in Jesus, were once contained in heaven but have become significant substance within the sphere of the earth. Such manifestations of the divine offer all who had dwelt in darkness and despair, deliverance and hope, to transform and empower life and service that transcend time and space (2 Cor. 5:17–19).

Jesus never concealed the expansion of the capacity of the people He called to follow Him. He used every possible opportunity to share this vital truth with those who followed Him. Commencing with the very first two men who forsook all to follow Him and culminating with the eleven He sent out into the world as witnesses of Him and all that He taught and accomplished, Jesus gave systematic teachings that encouraged an expectation of expansion in the capacity they possessed.

"Follow Me, and I will make you become fishers of men" (Mark 1:16) was the statement Jesus spoke to Simon and his brother Andrew when He called them away from their father and employer to make them His disciples. Their transformation and subsequent cultivation of capacity for partnership with Him in the mission of human redemption are very much envisaged in the call He gave to them. Therefore, it should not be surprising for us to read that He gave them the keys of the kingdom so that they could operate in the ministry of binding and loosing (Matt. 16:19).

In addition to such revelations, John accounted for Him telling them about the more outstanding works they would do because of what they would receive from the Father by praying in His name (John 14:12–14). Such teachings contain a variety of essential themes amongst which capacity expansion is once again affirmed. This is also evident in the final set of instructions He gave before He departed from the earth. As they assembled before Him on the Mount of Olives, He opened His mouth and reminded them of that one critical lesson which He taught them on previous occasions: "You shall receive power when the Holy Spirit has come upon you; and you shall be witnesses to Me" (Acts 1:8).

This blessing of the outpouring of the Holy Spirit was in addition to all that He gave them in teaching and example since the day He first called them to Himself. There is no apparent limit envisaged concerning their expansion in capacity for effective service in the redemption mission (Matt. 28:19–20). For the promised Holy Spirit, who indwells and abides with each believer who keeps His commandments (John 14:15–18), will teach "all things" and bring back to remembrance all that He shared previously about the Kingdom (John 14:26; 16:12–15). We note the idea of capacity expansion in the dual service that, according to Jesus, the Holy Spirit will fulfil in the lives of all who believe in Him and love Him. Besides providing new information about the kingdom and how best to serve its purpose in a world where the devil, demons, and sin are in operation, the Holy Spirit will help believers recall for consolation, hope, and faith, all that He gave previously in example and precepts. He accomplished all this to expand the capacity bestowed for an enriching experience in serving the love of God, both to the saved and the lost amongst humanity.

We would like to close this section with a more extensive reflection on the teaching Jesus gave in John 15:1–8, which we believe to be pertinent to capacity expansion.

> "I am the true vine, and My Father is the vinedresser. Every branch in Me that does not bear fruit He takes away; and *every branch* that bears fruit He prunes, that it may bear more fruit. You are already clean because of the word which I have spoken to you. Abide in Me, and I in you. As the branch cannot bear fruit of itself, unless it abides in the vine, neither can you, unless you abide in Me. "I am the vine; you *are* the branches. He who abides in Me, and I in him, bears much fruit; for without Me you can do nothing. If anyone does not abide in Me, he is cast out as a branch and is withered; and they gather them and throw *them* into the fire, and they are burned. If you abide in Me, and My words abide in you, you will ask what you desire, and it shall be done for you. By this My Father is glorified, that you bear much fruit; so, you will be My disciples."

One of the major themes of this passage is that of the value of word-based prayer. Prayer as a vital means for capacity expansion is extensively discussed in chapter 3 of this book, so we will restrict the nature of the reflection given to it at this point. However, expansion and productivity are very much at the heart of this teaching. Jesus highlighted that believers' connection to Him is pivotal to productivity and constitutes a critical feature of capacity expansion. Even as branches are dependent on the vine, to which they are connected for life and vitality, so are all who believe in Jesus dependent on Him for life and directed functions that amount to fruit-bearing. He was specific in both language and intention as He unequivocally declared this to His disciples, "I am the true vine; you are the branches. He who abides in Me, and I in him, bears much fruit; for without Me you can do nothing" (John 15:5).

Abiding in the Lord is a definite prerequisite for abundant life, good spiritual health, and productivity. Jesus explained to the disciples that to abide in Him has to do with His word abiding in them (John 15:7). In other words, people cannot claim that they abide in Jesus if their lifestyle bears no resemblance to the instructions He gave and the examples He displayed in service to God and humankind. What Jesus taught and practised concerning behavioural conduct towards God and humanity constitutes what His followers aspire for even as they serve God and people within a world where unclean spirits are in operation. Therefore, at the heart of this reciprocal abiding is a concern for growth in faith and the facilitation of such growth through devotional submission to the commands He gave. Importantly, abiding in Jesus and His word speaks of and demands much more than an accumulation of information that He is reported to have given.

Obedience is a critical factor, like the abiding that is advanced by Jesus in the passage under examination. This is consistent with the theme of obedience which He expounded on in the previous chapter of John's account of His life and ministry (John 14:15, 21, 23). Therefore, abiding in Jesus and His word speaks of a consistent walk of faith in the light of the word, or that of dwelling in and with the word in a way that demonstrates conformity to the vitality of its dynamic nature (John 6:63; Heb. 4:12).

Let us be careful also to note that abiding in Jesus and providing access of His word to the inner soul secures the attention of the Father and His expert service that affects longevity and more excellent fruit production (John 15:2). Neglect of intimacy with Jesus and rejection of His word results in expulsion from the kingdom of God and the ultimate demise of eternal fire (John 15:6).

The priority of intimacy with Jesus and obedience to His word is a continuous walk of faith which is undertaken in the light of the word of

God. This is also an indication of capacity expansion. It is the knowledge of the revealed will of God that is contained in the word which Jesus spoke that affords development in the faith capacity required for abiding in Him. Jesus presents this development in faith capacity as critical to fruit production. Therefore, it is not just in the capacity of the means of faith and the development of that faith, that the people of God should anticipate that increase. Fruit production, according to this teaching, is evidence of capacity expansion. Through the Word, which abides in the inner life of believers and by which our prayers are informed, fruit production is made possible.

Therefore, Jesus's teaching in John 15 reveals the interrelatedness between abiding in Him and His word, faith development, and its effectiveness in prayer to secure divine responses to specific requests, composed with desire for fruit production and the glory of God. Growth in fellowship with Jesus encourages and facilitates obedience to His teachings. This in turn aids the cultivation of faith which, when exercised in prayer, secures answers that amount to fruit production for the glory of God. This blessing—the development of our capacity for prevailing prayer and fruit production—is what Jesus desires for all His disciples. For us to want less is most definitely a sin!

Personal Assessment Tool

How might Jesus's growth in the wisdom of God and favour of both God and the people of His community encourage your capacity development for Ministry effectiveness?

---

3. Paul's Treatment of the Subject of Capacity Expansion and Development

Much is documented in the inspired scriptures for our learning regarding the growth and development of believers' faith. In particular, Paul punctuated his letters with passages that consider the expansive nature of the precious gift of faith believers received from the Lord. Such passages are specifically constructed, under the inspiration of the Holy Spirit, to bring the membership of Jesus's Church to the place of awareness and discovery concerning the potential increase there is to be obtained in the dynamic faith we have received. Some of these passages are listed below not just as evidence for the justification of the point in view but as a means of provoking intensive enquiry into some of the ways through which the people of God can grow and develop their capacity for delivering comprehensive and useful service here on earth.

Paul was aware of the need for the people of God to grow and develop the capacity they received from the Lord. He believed and promoted believers' embodiment of a robust victorious stance before the enemy of our souls, while being equally effective in the delivery of the vital ministry responsibilities that are intrinsic to bestowed spiritual gifts. We know this to be so from what the Holy Spirit inspired him to write in the following passages: 2 Corinthians 10:12–16, Ephesians 1:15–21, and Colossians 1:10. We have reflected on these in turn.

2 Corinthians 10:12–16

For we dare not class ourselves or compare ourselves with those who commend themselves. But they, measuring themselves by themselves, and comparing themselves among themselves, are not wise. We, however, will not boast beyond measure, but within the limits of the sphere which God appointed us—a sphere which especially includes you. For we are not overextending ourselves (as though *our authority* did not extend to you), for it was to you that we came with the gospel of Christ; not boasting of things beyond measure, *that is,* in other men's labours, but having hope, *that* as your faith is increased, we shall be greatly enlarged by you in our sphere, to preach the gospel in the *regions* beyond you, *and* not to boast in another man's sphere of accomplishment.

Paul speaks of the cherished hope he had for this and its eventual consequential effect on the work that he delivered about the specific point of the increase of faith among the Corinthian brethren. The increase of faith in the lives of the people he served is linked directly to the possible increase in the influence of the work he fulfilled. Growth in faith capacity and influence in ministry are tied together, primarily because they are interconnected aspects of the profound spiritual service that the apostle and the members of the Corinthian Church delivered, by virtue of the fact that they are both receptacles of the Holy Spirit and agents of His mighty workings (Acts 1:8; Rom. 8:9–11; 1 Cor. 12:3–11).

In what ways, then, do the increase of faith among the Christians in Corinth cause an increase in the work that the Lord sent Paul to deliver? Is it not in the fact that their expansion in faith constitutes a testimony that confirms the integrity and authenticity of Paul's calling and ministry? Such development in faith capacity can only serve to fuel the passion of the called and commissioned labourer. Even though the brethren in Corinth had developed a form of prejudicial complex against Paul (1 Cor. 3:1–8), he desired for them nothing besides their growth and development in the faith. This desire was anchored in and nurtured by the very Spirit who gave him his ministry and the message of the gospel of Christ, which he preached. Paul realised the intrinsic growth and development component of the capacity bestowed to the Corinthian believers. He mentioned this as something that positively impacted on his ministry. Notably, Paul did not allow the trivial scheming of carnal-minded men to distract him from the potential increase they experienced in faith as a direct result. Therefore, he did all that was necessary to eclipse what they had done to sabotage the furtherance of the Ministry of Jesus's Church. As a maturing and responsible Minister of grace, he redirected the Corinthian brethren to give focused attention to the work which they were called by the Lord to deliver for human salvation and the glory of His name.

There is much growth to be experienced in personal and collective faith capacity that amounts to the furtherance of the ministry of Jesus's Church in the earth. Realising this possibility can be most empowering for all who have the assurance of the call of God upon their lives. Therefore, the progress that Paul identified among the Corinthian brethren, as a significant contributing factor to his ministry, is one that should serve as a definite motivation for all who are engaged in the service of the Lord's Church. Only when Ministers who are committed to partnership Ministry with God, through the Spirit, come to such awareness will negative experiences, especially those encountered through the deeds and utterances of fellow believers, be appraised as tools by which to expect and experience an increase in both favour and ministry opportunity.

Ephesians 1:15–21

> Therefore I also, after I heard of your faith in the Lord Jesus and your love for all the saints, do not cease to give thanks for you, making mention of you in my prayers: that the God of our Lord Jesus Christ, the Father of glory, may give to you the spirit of wisdom and revelation in the knowledge of Him, the eyes of your understanding being enlightened; that you may know what is the hope of His calling, what are the riches of the glory of His inheritance in the saints, and what *is* the exceeding greatness of His power toward us who believe, according to the working of His mighty power which He worked in Christ when He raised Him from the dead and seated *Him* at His right hand in the heavenly *places,* far above all principality and power and might and dominion, and every name that is named, not only in this age but also in that which is to come.

In this passage, Paul intentionally expressed the desire he carried in his heart and mind for the development and maturity of the Christians in Ephesus. Their faith in Jesus Christ and sincere love for the saints, which are two of the hallmarks of those who have left the world and have become valued members of God's new creation community (Eph. 1:3–14, 2:1–13; 2 Cor. 5:17), are identified and affirmed. They are not just vital evidence of spiritual grace but are part of the foundation for growing and developing the gift of faith that the Lord bestowed upon them. The exhibition of these vital spiritual traits indicated that they had the capacity for growth in the things of the Spirit. They had the basics required for expansion and development. Paul prayed that additional spiritual grace would be given to them to know an increase in the substance of the faith and the manifestation of its efficacy. Because Paul was aware of the expansive and developmental nature of the grace of God in the life of the redeemed (Phil.

3:12–16), he took great delight in consistently praying that the Church in Ephesus would experience this. Desiring the increase of the people of God was seen by Paul as an essential responsibility that he did not want to ignore or abandon in the slightest!

Paul knew of some of the deeper depths and higher heights in Christ Jesus due to his maturity in the faith—a maturity predicated on his sacrificial response to the prophetic anointing that was upon him (Col. 1:19, 2:3, 9). Armed with such vital experiential knowledge, he intentionally set out to provoke the brethren in Ephesus to aspire to such places and become possessors of the knowledge available to all who attain them in Christ Jesus. The one prayer that he frequently offered on their behalf was that they would be filled with the "spirit of wisdom and revelation in the knowledge of God and for the eyes of their understanding to be enlightened". This prayer has "capacity to increase" written all over it!

The remainder of the prayer, which Paul prayed on their behalf, contains the type of response he expected God to deliver. He anticipates that believers would discover and grow in appreciation of "the hope to which God has called them". Acquiring knowledge about "the riches of the glory of His inheritance in the saints" is another of the expectations Paul believed his prayers would secure for the brethren in Ephesus. Furthermore, Paul hoped that his prayers would secure for believers the experiential knowledge of "the exceeding greatness of God's power". This is the power which God expressed in their behalf and "according to the working of His mighty power which He worked in Christ when He raised Him from the dead and seated *Him* at His right hand in the heavenly places, far above all principality and power and might and dominion, and every name that is named, not only in this age but also in that which is to come" (Eph. 2:21–23). Every one of these expectations offers something impactful to the capacity of the Ephesian brethren. They are all about enrichment, expansion in spiritual knowledge, faith development, and confident and competent participation in the delivery of the Ministry. Paul's prayer requests and their expected fulfilment are concerned with expanding the capacity that the Ephesian brethren received when they came to God and His kingdom through faith in Jesus Christ. These blessings are available to us too. As in the case of the Ephesian brethren—even so, it is for us—God gave them for the growth and development of the capacities we received from Himself. Let us claim them so we too will fulfil our Ministry and bring glory to our God and Father.

Colossians 1:9–12

> For this reason we also, since the day we heard it, do not cease to pray for you, and to ask that you may be filled with the knowledge of His will in all wisdom and spiritual understanding; that you may walk worthy of the Lord, fully pleasing Him, being fruitful in every good work and increasing in the knowledge of God; strengthened with all might, according to His glorious power, for all patience and longsuffering with joy; giving thanks to the Father who has qualified us to be partakers of the inheritance of the saints in the light.

This passage is reminiscent of the text we reflected on from the book of Ephesians earlier. Its message offers evidence that points to the fact that capacity expansion and development is a vital aspect of the experience of each disciple of the Lord Jesus Christ. What Paul desired for the brethren in Ephesus, and spent time seeking through intercession and supplication, is repeated in identical language concerning those comprising the Christian Fellowship, which he established in Colossae, in partnership with the Holy Spirit and other gifted Ministers.

After reflecting on the above three selected portions of scripture, we can conclude that Paul believed that the spiritual capacities believers received from the Lord carry an intrinsic expansion and development component. He saw his ministry as a tool given for its promotion amongst all believers. What we observe Jesus doing among the disciples, we now see the apostles replicating in diligent service to the Church. There is nothing else for us to do besides availing ourselves to the same order and standard which Jesus has so carefully laid out in His teaching. The responsive way Paul gave attention to all that Jesus exemplified and commanded speaks volumes about their importance in informing and facilitating the growth and development of the capacity received for victorious living and effective service. We have no other standard or calling besides that which the apostles received from Jesus and made available to us!

Personal Assessment Tool
What are some ways that Paul's treatment of the subject of capacity expansion and development might influence your growth and development as a Minister of grace for mentoring other believers?

4. Capacity Expansion and Development in Peter's Letters

Peter's letters are not without reference to the increase that those who believe in Jesus can expect to receive as they continue with Him in covenant communion. Although the first recipients of his letters were exposed continuously to mortal danger under the tyranny of the Roman emperor Nero, Peter's concern was not so much for their escape from such harsh realities but for their personal holistic salvation. However, God reserved this salvation in heaven for the faithful (1 Pet. 1:3–5). It is also one that has significant implications for how those who expect to receive its fullness, in the end, should live among themselves (1 Pet. 3:1–7, 4:7–11, 5:1–8) and also amongst those who persecute them (1 Pet. 2:11–25, 3:13–17, 4:12–19). All of this was contingent not so much on them believing in Jesus, despite its indispensable necessity for salvation. It was their aptitude for learning and applying the essentials of the faith under very challenging circumstances that Peter seems to emphasise.

The effectiveness of the faith that this believing community had in the Lord Jesus hinged on their willingness to become students of the Word.

Peter was deliberate and intentional about believers becoming students of the Word and how to live victorious lives and serve the purpose of the kingdom of God in the world. We first observed his passion for the Word when he stood with the other eleven apostles to address the Church in Acts 6:1–7 concerning internal challenges. The desire he had to see the word of God established in the lives of believers as an uncontested priority is expressed by him again with great intensification in 1 Peter 2:1–3, as he directed the recipients of his letter to become students of the Word.

Growth in the Word, which in essence is about capacity expansion, is required for faith development (Rom. 10:17) and correcting carnal behaviour (Eph. 4:17–32). Without the Word, no believer can reach the place of maturity in the life of the Spirit. Peter was well aware of this because he was a student in the school of Jesus when He delivered the vital teaching about the importance of the Word for salvation, effective praying, and productivity in service, in John 15:1–8. All that he expected from those he addressed in his letter regarding faith in Jesus Christ, service of love to each other, and remaining faithful to the mission of Christ amidst a hostile environment was possible only through the expansion of their God-given capacity in the power of the Spirit.

The continuation of carnal behavioural expression, which is an evident lack of submission to God, and which weakens and silences believers before the enemies, is the inevitable consequence of a lack of growth and development in the Word. This is the case because the Word, which is the staple diet for all who are born again, has found no place to abide and from which to flourish and give the expression of the efficacy of the intrinsic divine essence it contains (Isa. 55:10–11; John 1:1–3; Heb. 4:12). As a result of such lack, carnal behaviour will go unchecked, the means of faith will be absent, and the basis for unabashed confidence and the source of persistent spiritual authority will be non-existent.

The plan of capacity expansion for personal growth and development and Ministry effectiveness was something that Peter gave much more than a passing glance. It was a subject of importance to which he gave much attention insofar as giving it a place of significance in his second letter, even as he had done in the first. From the very outset of his second letter, we observe that believers' growth and development in the knowledge of God was an essential responsibility that appeared to be uppermost in Peter's mind. Peter's second message could be summarised as, "Do not neglect the agenda of personal development through the Word." As the Holy Spirit moved him to keep this plan at the forefront of believers' minds, he penned the following.

> Grace and peace be *multiplied* to you in the knowledge of God and of Jesus our Lord, as His divine power has given to us all things that *pertain* to life and godliness, through the knowledge of Him who called us by glory and virtue, by which have been given to us exceedingly great and precious promises, that through these you may be partakers of the divine nature, having escaped the corruption *that is* in the world through lust. (2 Pet. 1:2–4)

Peter used key terms such as *multiply* and *grow* to speak of Jesus's desire for the increase and maturity of believers in the life of the Spirit within His kingdom. Through the knowledge of God and Christ, believers can experience increased favour and peace while they live on the earth. These are two elements of our spiritual capacity in which we can expect to see an increase even as our knowledge of God and His Word increases. This is the very salvation for which Jesus prayed, before ascending the Cross: "That they may know You, the only true God, and Jesus Christ whom You have sent" (John 17:3). Increased knowledge of God and His Word affords spiritual insights. The people of God receive supernatural power to live through any trial and rise above any situation that threatens life and progress.

Following on from the establishment of the basics that believers need for growth and development, as citizens of the kingdom of God, Peter then directs his audience to become engaged in a seven-stage interconnecting developmental model of spiritual capacity. This is designed to progress the expansion of the capacity they received from the Lord through the Spirit. He prefixed these essential features of this development programme with the admonition "giving all diligence". Although we do not identify this as one of the seven principles in the model of capacity development, we cannot afford to overlook the value it holds for all concerned.

In effect, without due diligence, nothing can be achieved in the advancement of our faith. While faith is a gift bestowed by God through the dynamic activity of preaching (Rom. 10:17), its efficacy provides for the pursuit of all that is holy through the desires generated within the hearts and minds of those who have received the preached Word with understanding (Matt. 13:23). Due diligence is not a standalone process of activity generated out of a naturalistic mentality predisposed to self-promotion. It is the life of the Spirit by which the souls of believers become regenerated, and to which this dynamic factor of due diligence owes its existence. In effect it is a process of engagement that specifies objectives believers are to achieve. It is how its origin and effectual outworking are determined that truly defines its character. We can draw no other conclusion besides that which is consistent with the identity of the Sovereign God, who is Spirit (John 4:23), and who accomplishes all things in redemption concerning humankind by His Word and Spirit (Luke 1:26–38, 3:21–22, 4:1–2, 14; John 3:3–5; Heb. 9:14; Rom. 8:1–11; Acts 1:8; 2 Cor. 2:9–16). Therefore, this due diligence is not natural but spiritual. Unregenerated human beings do not determine it. It is a work of redemption that the Holy Spirit accomplishes by His creative might within the believer's surrendered life, for conformity to the perfect image of God, as expressed in Jesus Christ (John 1:14, 18; Rom. 8:29; Gal. 4:19).

We must also speak of the faith that Peter admonishes all believers to grow and develop as the base within which to anchor the respective seven spiritual capacity building-blocks outlined below. He instructs believers to add a variety of vital spiritual elements to the faith which God bestowed in grace to all who accept the preached word. But what are we to learn about this faith upon which Peter believes followers of Jesus Christ ought to be building?

When he wrote about faith being the bedrock upon which believers are to build, what Peter had in mind is not just belief, confidence, or trust that has its roots in mere human intellectual ability. This understanding of faith generally comes to mind whenever the term is used amongst church communities that do not understand the concept as it appears in the Holy Scriptures. In this instance, the emphasis is confined to how one becomes persuaded or convinced to exercise trust. The fundamental belief—the confidence or trust one exerts or holds to—is not what constitutes the emphasis Peter promotes. Importantly, it is the person of God—Father, Son, and Holy Spirit—and the self-revealing knowledge which they emit through the mighty works they accomplished in creation (Ps. 19:1–4; Rom. 1:16–20) and redemption (John 1:14–18; 2 Cor. 5:12–21). It is the knowledge of God's self-revelation that inspires and informs the belief, confidence, and trust generated in the minds and hearts of those to whom such revelations have come. It is the faith that has its foundation and expressive efficacy in God's identity and self-revelation that Peter called to believers' attention.[32]

Peter could impart such value-laden truths to believers because of the things he received as he listened to Jesus teach and pray (John 14:7–11, 17:1–3). The efficacy of the self-revelation of God—Father, Son and Holy Spirit (Matt. 16: 13–17)—affected Peter's holistic transformation and caused him to become like Jesus Christ, the embodiment of the word of God, driven to do all that is conceived and determined by the council of God.

Therefore, his admonition to "add to your faith" is not religious rhetoric spoken with the intent to secure grandeur for himself. Endeavouring to facilitate believers' growth and development in the holy faith was a responsibility of high priority that did not allow a moment to indulge the flesh in whatever derailing tactics it launched. Notably, "add to your faith" was explicitly stated to encourage believers to allow themselves to progress in the vitality of the faith. Receiving and possessing the knowledge of God, to the extent that the totality of their human character became transformed so that they would bear a definite resemblance to the image of God in Christ, is very much in view. Provoking believers to exercise themselves in grace intentionally, in the hope of attaining conformity to the high calling of God in Jesus Christ (Phil. 3:12–14), was a responsibility Peter received from the Lord Jesus (John 21:15–17). Encouraging believers to actively grow in the grace of God through the practice of applying themselves in study, prayer, and conversation undertaken, in the fellowship of Christ and that of the Holy Spirit (1 Cor. 1:9; 2 Cor. 13:14), is consistent with the responsibility which our Lord delegated to Peter. Finding him discharging his duty with passion and clarity amidst a multilayered hostile environment (1 Pet. 3:13–17, 5:8–12), speaks to his commitment to the mandate received from the Lord. The extent to which Peter grew and developed since the time of his demonstrated ignorance of Jesus's mission in the earth (Matt. 16:21–23) and his denial of Jesus on the eve of His crucifixion (Luke 22:47–62) provide invaluable insight in the transformational power of "the faith which was once for all delivered unto the saints" (Jude 3). We find it quite exciting and refreshing to see

---

[32]   W. E. Vine, *Vine's Concise Dictionary of the Bible* (Nashville: Thomas Nelson, 2005), 128.

an apostle of Peter's reputation honouring the commission he received and providing an example of vital importance to those upon whom God's mantle of Ministry for serving the current and the upcoming generations, has fallen.

Due diligence, then, is a devotional requirement that believers should exercise to ensure their development in the faith they have now come to possess through the knowledge of God and the Lord Christ Jesus (John 17:1–3). This exercise is not a work of the flesh but that of Spirit within the inner souls of regenerated people. It is yearning for and desiring the milk and food of the Word of God. According to Peter, divine favour and peace are contingent on the knowledge of God and the Lord Jesus Christ (2 Pet 1:2). The greater the knowledge of God and the Lord Jesus Christ, the greater the favour and peace that believers can expect to know and possess. The extent of the favour and the degree of peace which believers receive and possess are very much contingent on the degree to which believers grow in the knowledge of God and Christ Jesus, which is dynamic and developmental in its operational nature.

This is not to say that there is an inherent deficit in the actual knowledge which the identity and operations of God and Christ comprise and emit. Such a situation would be contradictory to the essence and nature of God and Jesus Christ. Because God is the eternal Spirit and Jesus Christ is the Living Word and very God (John 1:1–3; Rev 1:8), they have no lack and are therefore not in need of development or expansion. It is the extent to which the knowledge of God and Jesus Christ is allowed to settle within and positively affect believers' faculty and lived experience that we reference as capacity development.

Although Peter promised so much in his letters to all who possess the knowledge of God and Christ, it is by the discipline of diligent study, faithful prayer, and radical obedience that believers will obtain and retain the favour and peace which such knowledge produces. This process has to do with much more than committing key scripture passages to memory. As the case is, "without giving all diligence, there is no gaining any ground in holiness".[33] Therefore, this process of developing and practising diligence is one of the essential spiritual responsibilities that believers must prioritise. We now offer our attention to the specifics of this spiritual development programme outlined below in Figure 3.1, with brief commentary.

---

[33] Leslie F. Church, *Matthew Henry's Commentary on the Whole Bible* (Basingstoke: Marshall Morgan & Scott, 1960), 747.

Figure 3.1 Peter's Seven-Element Interconnecting Developmental Model of Spiritual Capacity (2 Peter 1:5–7)		
	Essential Feature	**The Value of Each in Expanding Capacity**
1.	**Virtue**	"Whatever procures pre-eminent estimation for a person or thing; hence, intrinsic eminence, moral goodness" and of "any particular moral excellence" or "where virtue is enjoyed as an essential quality in the exercise of faith".[34]
2.	**Knowledge**	From Greek *Gnosis*, denoting "seeking to know, an inquiry, investigation … especially of spiritual truth; or to know absolutely".[35]
3.	**Self-Control (Temperance)**	"The controlling power of the will under the power of the Spirit of God" prevents the abuse of spiritual gifts and ensures right response to God and the directives He gives.[36]
4.	**Perseverance**	"To continue steadfastly in a thing and give unremitting care to it."[37] *Patience* is the term used in the King James Version (KJV).

---

[34] W. E. Vine, *Vine's Expository Dictionary of New Testament Words* (Massachusetts: Hendrickson, 1992), 1212–1213.

[35] Ibid., 641.

[36] Ibid., 1137.

[37] Ibid., 89 (860). The verb *Proskarteresis*, which is akin in meaning with *Proskartereo*.

5.	**Godliness**	"To be devoted; piety, which is characterised by a Godward attitude, does that which is well-pleasing to Him."[38]
6.	**Brotherly Kindness**	"Denotes a brother, or near kinsman; in the plural, a community based on identity of origin or life; love of the brethren."[39]
7.	**Love**	"Describes the attitude God has toward His Son; it's also used by God to convey His will concerning believers' attitude one to another and toward all men."[40]

Virtue is the first of the seven elements in the capacity expansion programme that Peter directed his audience to embrace and learn. Because his intended audience already had faith by the truth of the Word that was preached to them—thus bringing them into a relationship with God through faith in Jesus by the Holy Spirit—Peter directed them to allow this very Word-producing faith to express the vitality of its nature through their every thought and utterances, and the prevailing attitude and deeds. Because the faith which comes by hearing the Word of God is by nature holy, powerful, and transformational in its effect, the pre-eminent estimation is that its very presence will become evident wherever it abides. Peter wanted the brethren to exercise their faith and receive all that it secures from God for righteousness amidst their harsh reality and eternity.

Knowledge is to be added to virtue—a virtue which is already anchored in the precious faith that has its foundation in the identity of God and the faithful Word He gives. This is not human-generated knowledge but that which is unique because it comes through intentional, investigative engagement, which is conducted under the direction and guidance of the

---

38   Ibid., 502.

39   Ibid., 156–157.

40   Ibid., 702–703.

Holy Spirit. This could be the intention of Peter, who is very aware that vital knowledge which brings about transformation and affords faith-generating power, comes from the Spirit of God and not so much through the mere exercise of the natural human intellectual competence (Matt. 16:13–23). This knowledge is the substance of God's self-revelation, which becomes the possession of believers who encounter and experience Him within the context of our lived reality.

The direct connection between virtue and knowledge must be readily perceived, willingly accepted, and faithfully cherished as that which exists between the Word of God and faith, if one is to apprehend such precious knowledge. The particular expertise with which we are here concerned is revealed and obtained as a direct result of the virtue produced when faith is exercised. There is a unique spiritual knowledge intrinsic to the production of virtue through the exercise of faith in the Lord, based on the precious promises He gives. While this knowledge conforms to God's revelation, as documented in the scriptures, it is different primarily because it is acquired whenever faith is exercised amidst the lived experiences of believers. Because this knowledge is generated through the exercise of faith amidst believers' lived experiences—the faith generated and authenticated by the Holy Scriptures—it is therefore valid and reliable.

We would also like to note that acquiring such precious knowledge requires believers to give adequate reflection to the exercise of their faith amidst lived experiences. Despite having received the miraculous manifestation of God's power through the exercise of faith in His Word, believers must prepare to think through the enacted process under the tutelage of the Holy Spirit and in communal conversation with fellow sojourners. By doing this, the vital knowledge required for becoming temperate will become evident, and the occasion of the miracle will not become a memory which is recalled purely for nostalgia. Being reflective is critical to the process of expanding the knowledge capacity that the Spirit calls each believer to achieve in God through faith in Jesus Christ. Thinking about how the Lord works and how such mighty works expose and nullify demonic and natural hindrances to personal and community development in spiritual faith operations, are central to the reflection that we are here advancing.

Self-control or temperance is the next element of development in Peter's seven-stage programme for capacity expansion. Without this, abuse of power and gifts is almost inevitable amongst the community of faith. Growth in faith, virtue, and knowledge can lead to great disaster if believers do not manage it appropriately. Hence, the knowledge acquired through the exercise of faith and the discipline of judicious enquiry must be utilised by believers not to discourage inquirers but to enlighten others in accord with the directive previously given in 1 Peter 4:10–11. W. E. Vine states that self-control follows "knowledge", suggesting that what believers learnt should be practised. Therefore, practising what is known is a failproof plan for eclipsing the appeal of an egocentric disposition and the abuse of others associated with it. Being self-controlled is the most profound and compelling virtue in spiritual service and warfare. It affords unreserved compliance to the leading of the Spirit and keeps the welfare of others at an optimum level on a Minister's list of priority.

Peter advances ***perseverance*** as the next necessary element identified for development for believers' productive operations in the knowledge of the Lord Jesus Christ. Perseverance has nothing to do with being passive or static; neither is it about quietly waiting on the Lord to bring about some mighty deliverance (rescue or escape) whenever we are tested or tempted. At the heart of this vital spiritual virtue is the task of continual engagement in the service of the Lord amidst persecution. The reality of the persecution that the recipients of Peter's letters faced brings into focus the vitality of the message of continuity in faith, in his usage of the term perseverance. It was amidst this context of fierce trials and the potential for apostasy that Peter explained the vitality of perseverance. All that believers accrued in faith, virtue, knowledge, and temperance would be of no effect if endurance were absent. Believers have the evidence of the power of God's precious promises stored within their minds and have witnessed their efficacy amidst the various trying experiences encountered in life. This blessing allows believers to view persevering, not as a burden, but the very means of securing for ourselves and others the promised salvation that will never fade away (Matt. 24:3–14).

Perseverance is the power of the grace of God, bestowed in the souls of the redeemed by the Holy Spirit, through the life-giving and creative Word of God. It affords believers the courage required to continue steadfastly in devotional obedience to all that God commands with the understanding and assurance of an eternity with Him. Perseverance is a force for good in believers' lives. It is a testimony that attests to believers' denial of the flesh, the forsaking of the world, and persistent resistance against the wiles of the devil. In effect, perseverance is a path of suffering that comes about primarily because of believers' expressed willingness to pay the cost of authentic discipleship to Jesus Christ, even as He demanded in Matthew 16:24–27. Therefore, perseverance does not come about because we can provide some explanations of what it could mean. Only those who have gone through the gauntlet of self-denial and know the bittersweet experience of following Jesus with their cross can speak about the vitality of perseverance as a virtue and not just as an experience of suffering. Having reached such a place in the journey of faith puts believers in a position of strength to surrender entirely to the Spirit for guidance into the other stages in the capacity expansion programme.

Godliness is the fifth of the seven-element capacity expansion programme in which Peter called believers to become fully engaged. While godliness is a character trait of the redeemed life, it is against the backdrop of ungodliness that its beauty is made to shine profoundly. Of the value of godliness in believers' life, the celebrated expositor Matthew Henry says,

> When Christians bear afflictions patiently, they get an experimental *knowledge of the loving-kindness of their heavenly Father*, and hereby they are brought to the child-like fear, and reverential love wherein true holiness consists.[41]

Interestingly, Peter paired godliness with affliction. This paring is not to promote the idea that without affliction, godliness is not possible. He did this to explain that by affliction, believers are brought to the place of utter dependency on the Lord, which in effect provides the opportunity for realising the vitality of the godly nature we obtained when we believed in Jesus and received the gift of the Holy Spirit by whom we are born again. Submitting to the Lord amidst the reality of trial, persecution, and affliction should not be perceived as allowing others to disadvantage us. However, it is as Peter stated in his first letter: "For he who has suffered

---

[41]   Matthew Henry, 1960, p. 747.

has ceased from sin, that he should live no longer the rest of his time in the flesh and for the lust of men, but for the will of God" (1 Peter 4:1–2). Being dead to sin and its appeal and living according to the will of God is indeed godliness.

Being conformed to God's image in Christ Jesus amidst the trials and afflictions of life is a necessary part of the capacity expansion programme that we too should set ourselves to embrace. Therefore, the challenges that we face as we seek to honour the Lord with our lives should not find us seeking the pathway of cowards and those who are pretentious. Instead, they should serve the purpose of stripping from us all the rags of the flesh, so that the new nature we possess in Christ Jesus, through the gift of God's grace, would so shine through until the Father sees His reflection perfectly framed in us!

Brotherly kindness is the sixth element of development that those who are born again should endeavour to cultivate. All that believers possess in their expansive essence is to be offered in service to benefit the entire community to which each believer belongs. Brotherly kindness allows each believer to become responsible custodians and proficient dispensers of God's bestowed grace, in a manner that facilitates the call of God for believers' maturity to be achieved by the Spirit, through the ready and willing participation of each redeemed soul. This vital truth, which has already been put forth in 1 Peter 4:10–11, is here reinforced with the directive to make brotherly kindness one of the spiritual proficiencies in which believers are to experience growth and development. This expectation is consistent with the very purpose for which God called believers from darkness and afforded them a place of significance amongst His people (1 Pet. 2:9–10).

Brotherly kindness is asking for much more than a token gesture from one believer to another. Each believer should serve others out of the supply which is received from the Lord. For example, those who have amassed spiritual power through faith in the Word, virtue from the knowledge which the Spirit affords, the vitality of self-control from practising the truth of the Word, and the acquisition of patience through perseverance and godliness as its reward should serve each other out of this abundant blessing. Therefore, the type of service delivered by one believer to another is an indicator by which to judge not just the quality of that which is bestowed but how bestowed grace has been received, understood, and shared. Whatever we serve and how we serve is one sure way of accounting for the extent to which we have received and grown in the various capacities we have received from the Lord. See Philippians 2:1–11 for an example of what this may look like in practice.

Love (charity) is the seventh element in the list of capacity expansion directives given by Peter. Interestingly, love is the last of the seven elements in this spiritual developmental structure. When we consider that the priority of love trumps everything that one may do in living and serving, we need to ascertain the purpose for the place it occupies within the spectrum of the capacity expansion and development elements given by Peter.

Having obtained power by which other vital spiritual characteristics become evident through spiritual ministration, operating in such an authority without the motivation of love is empty and devoid of enduring spiritual fervour. Having this gift of love takes the Ministers of God to a place of service where they "express the essential nature of God, 1 John 4:8".[42] Biblical spiritual Ministry is not predicated on the familial relationships we may form as the principle of brotherly kindness may suggest. Neither is it based on the fact that Ministers can do certain works because they have power and knowledge. Adding love to the constellation of capacities that believers obtained through grace and submission ensures that believers deliver Ministry not under the guise of the flesh but through the power of God's sacrificial love. Therefore, believers serving others from the standpoint of their need, and not based on mere emotional attachment, is what God's bestowed love endeavours to achieve.

We chose to give the last words in this section to the renowned Irish preacher William Barclay, who commented on the nature of the love which Christ directed His disciples to serve to all people (Matt. 5:43–45) and the particular manner in which it is to be.

> This is what Christian love is. It is an attitude to other people. It is the set of the will toward others. It is the attitude of a good will that cannot be altered, a desire for men's good that nothing can kill. Quite clearly, it is not simply a response of the heart; this is

---

42   Vine, *Expository Dictionary of New Testament Word*, 703.

not an emotional reaction; this is an act of the will. In this, it is not merely our heart that goes out to others; it is our whole personality. And this is why it can be commanded and demanded of us.[43]

Having taken unto ourselves Peter's seven-stage interconnected developmental programme, we should be at a place to show love and demonstrate that we are indeed children of our Father (Matt. 5:43–48). This means to have a good conscious intention to benefit others irrespective of their cultural, political, or religious connections or affiliations, and all the other value-laden categories generally used to form barriers and underpin prejudicial and oppressive practices. This is the kind of outcome that becomes possible whenever we allow our capacity to grow through submission to the work of the Spirit.

Personal Assessment Tool
What lessons have you learned from the place of importance that Peter gave to the divine plan of capacity expansion that you can use to minister to believers who are living in hostile circumstances?

---

[43]   William Barclay, *Ethics in a Permissive Society* (Glasgow: Collins Found Paperbacks, 1971), 34.

5. The Promise of Capacity Expansion in the Epistles of John

We now come to the final element in this chapter. It is an evaluation of John's treatment of the subject of capacity growth and development. It is vital to point out that we do not intend to draw upon the contents of John's Gospel at this juncture. We believe that the content of John's Gospel differs somewhat to those contained in the three letters which he wrote. The Gospel is more an account of the eternal personhood of Jesus Christ—the living Word of God incarnated—and the life and ministry he lived and served. The letters or epistles contain a perspective that echoes his understanding of the core message of the Gospel. For example, the intended audience of the Gospel seems to be the unsaved population of the world (John 20:30), whilst the epistles are written to believers (1 John 1:1–4; 2 John 1–2; 3 John 1). It is the way he shared his interpretation and understanding of that vital message, in his direct dealings with those he loved and served, that is of importance here.

We can identify the presence of the capacity expansion plan from the opening address to his readers at the beginning of the first of the three epistles. He wrote about fellowship (1 John 1:3) and the fullness of joy derived from what he shared (1 John 1:4). This fellowship that John wrote about is the one which delivers from darkness (1 John 1:6) and testifies about cleansing from sin (1 John 1:7). This fellowship is therefore one of deliverance and empowerment. It allows for one's rescue from sin and darkness and all that is associated with them and for one's participation in every blessing that the knowledge of Jesus Christ provides. Fellowship with the Father and the Son, communion with believers, and fullness of joy are some of the many blessings that the knowledge of Christ Jesus affords. This knowledge is about how to live in obedience to Christ (1 John 2:3–14), how to overcome the wicked one (1 John 3:4–9), how to discern between the Holy Spirit and demonic spirits (1 John 4:1–6), and the vital assurance of eternal life in God through faith in Jesus Christ (1 John 5:1–13).

John accounted for numerous blessings in the first epistle that can take us a great deal of time to numerate, study, and absorb. This is a project that we need to embark upon to expand our capacity in the Word for victorious living and effective service. However, the process by which such blessings become transposed from being ideas documented in the Bible to substantive measurable facts in the life and service of believers should be our focus. It is only through the expansion of our capacity that these things are made possible. This expansion in capacity, which affords victorious living and impactful service, is predicated entirely upon the Word of God and the work of the Spirit. Hence the affirmative declaration from John: "And these things we write to you that your joy may be full" (1 John 1:4).

The plan of capacity growth and development is not explicit in the second epistle, but it is in the third epistle. Here we find that John addresses the subject in a different language from the first epistle. It is the word *prosper* that he used in this instance, which means "to help on one's way".[44] By implication, it has to do with supporting someone to enable them to complete a journey successfully or to maintain a position of victory or influence for the duration of an allotted period.

John knew the challenging circumstances which existed in the church where Gaius generally assembled and the quality, strength, and confidence he needed to maintain his testimony, the ministry of love which he served to the brethren and his witness of Jesus Christ to the unsaved world (3 John 9–10). He wasted no time expressing the intent of his heart and prayer for his increase so that he would be in a position to be more effective in what he was known to do (3 John vs. 3–8). He wrote: "Beloved, I pray that you may prosper in all things and in health, just as your soul prospers" (3 John v. 3).

This portion of scripture does not constitute an evident or specific promise from the Lord, but it does offer some vital insights that speak to the intention of the sovereign Lord to increase the people He established in the earth for the glory of His name. It is of interest to note that this indication of capacity expansion is a writer's wish. As the context reveals, John desired that Gaius would experience development on a holistic level and not just in a one-dimensional manner. He hoped that Gaius would experience growth and increase in all things. The phrase *all things* indicate the entire spectrum of Gaius's affairs, including his life, family, business, and ministry. John wanted to see this godly man flourish in every area of his life because he knew the benefit that he endeavoured to bring to the Body of Christ and the witness of the Church He established in the earth.

---

44   W. E. Vine, *Vine's Concise Dictionary of the Bible*, 293–294.

Let us be careful to note that the prosperity that John hoped that Gaius would experience also extended to his physical being. As his family and business affairs increased, even so, John anticipated that Gaius' physical health would be enhanced so that he would live to enjoy the increase of all things; this is inclusive of more excellent service and more outstanding results.

The scale or standard for measuring the increase that John desired for Gaius in all things is identical to that which his soul enjoys through communion with God and Christ in the Spirit (John 14:23). Believers' inner life is transformed and empowered by the indwelling Spirit, thus causing "rivers of living water" to flow from within (John 7:38). By this power, God can "do exceedingly abundantly above all that we ask or think" (Eph. 3:20). As a direct result of God's engagement with believers, we experience supernatural power in the entirety of our lived experience on the earth. This inner spiritual working of God is to increase our physical, spiritual, intellectual, and financial capacity to produce works of excellence that positively affect and enhance the welfare of many, for the ultimate glory of His name.

But is this not a personal wish that John had for Gaius? Should this be treated as vital evidence that adds value to the proposed idea that it is God's will to expand the capacity of the people called by His name? These questions can only be answered with a resounding yes, because John was not expressing a wish per se but, accounting to Gaius, the type of prayers he offered before God on his behalf. John asked God to bless Gaius with the kind of increase in the above verses as routine. John's commitment to pray this way reveals that believers' prosperity is very much a considered and recognised dimension in the redemptive work of the Lord in the here and now!

Summary Statement and Personal Evaluation

The various portions of the scriptures chosen and reflected on in the earlier discussions indicate the vitality of capacity expansion as a sacred responsibility. Identifying this teaching at multiple places in the Holy Scriptures is remarkable. Such evidence highlights the significance of capacity expansion in the redemptive work of God amongst believers. The discovery of such a body of evidence should therefore serve to stimulate excitement in our inner being for renewed interest in personal development and greater availability for service in the Church of our Lord Jesus Christ. Our privileged responsibility, in light of such irrefutable biblical evidence, is one that demands a threefold response.

The first responsibility is to carefully read through the passages of scriptures highlighted and explored in this work. This reading should be done in a meditative fashion to allow each word, each phrase, and each portion to penetrate the totality of one's mentality and inner world. The extent to which their spiritual substance becomes the content of the inner life and the fuel for our motivation in devotional worship, intercessory prayer, and sacrificial service is dependent on the time we are willing to give to such an exercise.

The second responsibility that each believer should then attend to is learning to pray according to the Word of God. Having received the Word of God and abiding in its vital essence, believers are then required to pray, asking the Father to bring into observable manifestation the complete substance of the life essence contained in each word. As we abide in the Word, we pray those prayers that meet the condition for the release of the miracle-working grace of the Father. This is not wishful thinking but the very process that Jesus dictated to the disciples in John 15:1–8.

The third responsibility that believers are to fulfil, in light of the body of evidence that points to the plan of God for the increase of the capacity which He bestowed to each of us through grace, **is that of becoming engaged in programmes and services geared at facilitating capacity expansion and development in others.** While it is good to realise the privilege that we have for capacity increase and development, we should seek to use all the opportunities available for the full realisation of the hope which the Holy Spirit ministers to us by the Word of God. By pursuing these essentials, we ensure that we are not engaging in another talking shop but a personally transformational and ministerially effective service. These were the very outcomes that Paul had in mind when He directed Timothy to be diligent to present himself approved of God, a worker who does not need to be ashamed, rightly dividing the word of truth (2 Tim. 2:15).

Capacity expansion is not a theme of inconsequential operation for the people of God. It is grounded in biblical theology and should therefore receive much more than a passing glance. It should be the ambition of every child of God—especially those who have announced their call to service in leadership in the Church of the Lord Jesus Christ—to heed the direction which Paul gave Timothy. It is not good enough for spiritual leaders to confine themselves solely to the learning that their initial faith formation training provides. While such knowledge is vital in establishing a solid foundation, the objective is to grow and develop and not just occupy such a space as persons suffering from arrested development.[45] The call of God is one that is specifically associated with growth and development. Therefore, spiritual leaders should not occupy a place of developmental restriction that impedes the growth and development of the very people who have been entrusted to them by the Holy Spirit, for care and supervision (Acts 20:28; 1 Cor. 12:4–11).

Know What You Believe[46] and *Know Why You Believe*[47] are not just works of apologetic significance to be celebrated in honour of a profound scholarly defender of our common faith. They constitute vital evidence of time spent in prayer; time spent studying the scriptures, and time spent delivering service to others. These were not services undertaken merely for exercising the intellect. They were processes geared at growing and developing divinely bestowed capacity. Giving the word of God to fellow believers and those who are yet in the world requires an understanding of effective teaching processes and learning styles. Understanding the socio-political context within which the audiences we serve live their lives, is also valuable. These are some of the essential values that the works of Paul E. Little, identified earlier, promote as worthy aspirations for everyone who serves in the Ministry of Jesus's Church. We can acquire none of these things without applying ourselves to a variety of learning processes. In essence, none of us can effectively serve unless we are prepared to grow, change, and develop. And this is what capacity expansion is about!

---

[45] Bradley C. Taber-Thomas, Erik W. Asp, Michael Koenigs, Matthew Sutterer, Steven W. Anderson, and Daniel Tranel, "Arrested Development: Early Prefrontal Lesions Impair the Maturation of Moral Judgement", *Brain* 137, no. 4 (April 2014), 1254–1261, https://doi.org/10.1093/brain/awt377.

[46] Paul E. Little, *Know What You Believe* (London: Scripture Union, 1973).

[47] Paul E. Little, *Know Why You Believe, Fourth Edition* (Downers Grove, IL., IVP, 2000).

An Evaluation of Personal Learning

At this stage, we encourage you to take some time out and reflect on the material studied so far. Consider how the ideas of capacity growth and development might apply in your discipleship journey. The following personal assessment tool intends to aid in this time of reflection.

Personal Assessment Tool
In what ways might John's desire for Gaius inform your attitude and service to increase those for whom you have responsibility and oversight?

Personal Assessment Tool
How might you use the knowledge you have gained from your study of this chapter to help your church organisation promote the value of supporting established Ministers and Ministerial candidates to give time and attention to personal capacity growth and development?

CHAPTER 4

Strategies for Increasing Capacity

> Godly people are disciplined people. It has always been so. Call to
> mind some heroes of church history—Augustine, Martin Luther,
> John Calvin, John Bunyan, Susanna Westley, George Whitefield,
> Lady Huntingdon, Johnathan and Sarah Edwards, Charles
> Spurgeon, George Muller—they were all disciplined people. In
> my own pastoral and Christian experience, I can say that I've
> never known a man or woman who came to spiritual maturity
> except through discipline. Godliness comes through discipline.[48]

The expressed intention of the Lord God concerning the expansion and
development of all who believe in Jesus and afforded a special gift of
power to become His children (John 1:12–13) can be understood by the
vital strategies which have been given in grace to all through the mighty
workings of the Holy Spirit. The calling of believers to become intimately
entwined with the word of God (Deut. 8:3; Josh. 1:8; John 15:7; 1 Pet.
2:1–3), to "pray without fainting or respite" (Luke 18:1; 1 Thess. 5:17), in
the power of the Holy Spirit (Rom. 8:10–11, 26; Eph. 6:17–20), and to
be engaged in spiritual supervision (Exo. 18:1–27; 1 Pet. 5:5; Tit. 2:1–8)
are all for growing and becoming mature, both as children of God and
committed proficient servants in the mission of the Church.

---

[48] Donald S. Whitney, *Spiritual Disciplines for the Christian Life* (Colorado:
NavPress, 1991), 17.

Our expansion and development in divinely bestowed capacities is a high priority in God's mission of redemption. Becoming efficient in the ministry of grace is not a responsibility left to believers to discover and manage. Because our efficiency in Ministry is determined by the grace that God bestows (John 15:5–8; Rom 12:3), the process of becoming aware of what is to be done and the means by which this is to be executed are responsibilities that God manages (Acts 1:8; 1 Cor 12:7–11). This is worked out through God's redemption activity and the partnership He establishes with the faithful community here on earth. Jesus's response to the disciples' question concerning the particular manner in which truth is revealed to them, in comparison to the concealing approach He took when dealing with unbelievers (Matt. 13:1–10), speaks volumes about the developmental plan that is at the heart of the mission of human redemption. He noted that "it is given to you to know the mysteries of the kingdom of heaven, but to them, it has not been given" (Matt. 13:11–17).

This developmental ambition is recognised and accounted for by Paul in his letters to the Corinthian and the Ephesian congregations as one of the objectives of the redemptive mission of God. To the Corinthians church, he wrote: "But the manifestation of the Spirit is given to each for the profit of all" (1 Cor. 12:7a). He then wrote this to the Ephesians: "And He Himself gave some to be apostles, some prophets, some evangelists, and some pastors and teachers, for the equipping of the saints, for the work of the ministry, for the edifying of the body of Christ ... according to the effectual working by which every part does its share and causes growth of the body for the edifying of itself in love." (Eph. 4:11–16).

The Lord ordained believers' growth and development. God expects all who come into His family to become proficient in the faith. This expectation of divine mastery gives convincing evidence and vital expression of the intrinsic significance we possess as God's special people who live for the glory of His name (1 Pet. 2:9–10).

Having laid the groundwork above, we will now discuss six tried and tested strategies for growing and expanding the capacity which the Lord has bestowed on every believer, which consists of (1) reading, (2) praying, (3) peer-conversation, (4) spiritual supervision, (5) reflective practice, and (6) spiritual tutelage. We will demonstrate how useful the spiritual disciplines we practised over the years enable our personal and collective capacity expansion and development. Indeed, these are vital tools for facilitating individual and communal growth and development and should be accorded the respect and recognition they deserve. Critically, the goal is that we all come to maturity as children of God and Ministers of grace and not just persons possessing a great degree of technical knowledge about the spiritual edification process.

1. Reading (New and Old Material)

Sir Frances Bacon is credited with the authorship of this well-known saying: "Reading makes a full man."[49] William Delaney says of reading, "Extensive reading fills the mind with information and ideas which inspire and provide for further thought and lead to new ideas."[50] Together, these affirmations of the value of reading indicate possible benefits for those established to deliver leadership in the Church of Jesus Christ.

One of the sure ways for disciples of the Lord Jesus Christ to increase their capacity is by reading the Word of God. Workers in the Church of Jesus Christ should never be lacking in this area of spiritual service as "God's fellow workers" (1 Cor. 3:9) are specifically instructed to make the written Word their staple diet (1 Pet. 2:1–3; 2 Pet. 3:18). The useful instruction given in Deuteronomy 8:3 reveals the indispensable vitality of the Word of God in believers' lives as an essential means for the expansion of divinely bestowed capacity. Let us note that it is by the Word of God that life is sustained and given the power for longevity (John 1:1–5). The sustenance of this life and its actual longevity have capacity increase written all over it. It is by the inherent life-generating essence of the Word of God that those who believe in Jesus and have obtained the power to become children of God (John 1:12–13) and members of His household (Eph. 2:19). The efficacy of this life enables those who possess it

---

[49] https://www.enotes.com/homework-help/what-did-sir-francis-bacon-mean-when-he-said-465148, accessed 24 Aug. 2020.

[50] William Delaney, "What Did Sir Francis Bacon Mean When He Said 'Reading Makes a Full Man; Conference a Ready Man; and Writing an Exact Man'?" *eNotes Editorial*, 6 December 2013, https://www.enotes.com/homework-help/what-did-sir-francis-bacon-mean-when-he-said-465148 accessed 23 January 2021.

to successfully navigate the obstacles of this earthly existence and overcome the corrupting and debilitating force of the cunning craftiness of the evil seen and encountered in it.

Additional insights about the cumulative power of the Word of God in capacity expansion and development are presented in other portions of the inspired scriptures. The directive given in Joshua 1:8 does not come with an inference for poetic indulgence. It is not for recitation that this directive is preserved and presented to all succeeding generations of believers. By this directive, God provides a vital strategy for believers to maintain a holy walk before His presence and resource for sustained prosperity and success in living and serving. The Holy Spirit reiterates the directive of Joshua 1:8, for our benefit, in Psalm 1. God also provided explicit instructions to His people in Psalm 1, concerning one of the vital means of expanding the capacity they possess in a world where much evil is in operation (Rom. 1:18–32; 1 Pet. 5:8).

According to Psalm 1, an ardent and determined desire for the things of God is sufficient to make one wise to the wiles of the enemy. It makes one relentless in the pursuit of the path of life, which obedience to the Word secures. This strategy is the same spiritual grace given to all believers by the Lord God to discern ungodly operations, to resist them with courage and wisdom, and to give oneself to loyal devotional service to the will of the Lord. In this vital portion of the inspired scriptures, another example is provided concerning how the capacity we received from the Lord can expand within our current times.

But the development of our spiritual and intellectual capacity through time spent with the inspired Word of God is very much dependent on the approach we adopt, whenever we come to the Word of God. The answers we provide to the following questions will offer us valuable insight into the prospect of reducing or increasing our spiritual and intellectual capacity for effective engagement in life and service, as disciples of the Lord Jesus Christ.

With what attitude and expectation do we come to God's Word? In what voice and through what lens do we read the written Word of God? Do we read the Word of God as a historical novel—a story that tells us about other people and their life journey—or do we read it as God's self-revelation and His delivering works amongst His human creation? Do we read the written Word of God as an instruction manual that informs our understanding of our origin and identity? Do we gain from the contents of the Holy Scriptures a sense of our ordained purpose, and how we should expedite it within the current climate of the world? Do we gain an understanding of the cherished hope of the destiny that is secured for everyone who believes in God through Christ Jesus by the Spirit, whenever we read the scriptures? Do we read the Word of God as that which makes one wise? Do we accept the contents of the Holy Scriptures as that which is inspired by God and is therefore "profitable for doctrine, for reproof, for correction, for instruction in righteousness", and as that which is to make the man of God "complete and thoroughly equipped for every good work" (2 Tim. 3:16–17)?

Capacity expansion and development are amongst the core insights offered to believers in 2 Timothy 3:16–17. We want to highlight this insight so everyone can note the critical value it produces within the life and ministry of men and women involved in the service of Jesus's Church. Consequently, let us note that by increasing our knowledge, insights, and understanding of our capacities, through time in the Word, we locate ourselves as proficient Ministers of grace in every context of life. Importantly, it is by the knowledge of the dynamic Word of God that the Ministers of God become "complete and thoroughly equipped for every good work". There is no substitute for the Word of God!

The attitude in which we come to the Spirit-inspired scriptures determines how we read and receive its sacred, liberating, and empowering contents. So critical is our perspective on the Word that it determines what we receive for life and ministry from its contents. It also informs the mindset in which we face the world and the various challenges common to all who live in it. There is also the small matter of the specifically planned situations that the devil directs against the people who are called by the Lord Jesus Christ. How we respond to these realities is contingent upon the attitude we bring to the Word of God. Our overcoming of evil and our continuous success in spiritual warfare are dependent on the attitude to which we approach the Word of God.

The reading undertaken by Christian leaders should not be restricted to the written Word of God, but nothing should replace the priority of the Word! Many insights are available to spiritual leaders from books written about the Word and the impact of the Word in the lives and ministries of faithful servants of the Lord. Biblical books and theological dictionaries provide tremendous value to those who desire to understand the message of the Bible better. However, these books may be limited in their scope, to the lives and the intellect of those who have written them. There are blessings of joy and empowerment available to those who read the Word of God, as contained in the canon of the scriptures, that cannot be derived from reading books written about the Bible. Servants of God should be positioned to distinguish between the respective value of reading the scriptures and books written about them. Therefore, the duty of reading the scriptures, not just texts which are written about them, is one that is commanded (Deut. 6:6; Josh. 1:8; 1 Pet. 2:2) and which we should not compromise. The pre-eminent position that the psalmist gave to the Word of God in Psalm 119 and that which the apostles demonstrated during the early days in the life of the Church (Acts 6:2) speak to the attitude and the desire those currently occupying positions of leadership in the Church should demonstrate toward the written Word of God.

Despite emphasising the importance of reading and studying as disciplines for enhancing capacity growth and development amongst Christian Ministers, we are in no way advocating that every person who occupies a leadership role in the Church of the Lord Jesus Christ should hold a PhD in theology. This would not be in keeping with the teaching that is offered by Paul in Romans 12:3–8, 1 Corinthians 12:5–11, and Ephesians 4:11–13 concerning the "measure of grace" and of "the gift which is given by the Holy Spirit" to those He established in particular offices and ministries in the Body of Christ. Furthermore, such an inference would reduce the role and work fulfilled by dynamic servants of the Lord, such as the austere Elijah and Amos, and relegate their work to a place of inferior status, particularly when compared with the eloquence of the learned Isaiah and Jeremiah.

The point of importance that we are here advancing is that each Minister of grace should possess that compelling and driving ambition to have a fuller knowledge of the role or office in which the Holy Spirit established them. Exerting energy through academic rigour, peer conversation, and reflective praying is critical to developing and honing those skills that are needful to discharge the responsibilities of their role or office effectively. Paul instructed Timothy to study to become effective in managing his ministry's duties, to the intent of justifying the call of the Lord upon his life (2 Tim. 2:15). It was not with the intention that he should pursue a doctoral degree that Paul gave this critical instruction. He was more concerned about a scholarship that provided evidence of understanding of the kingdom of God and the essentials with which it is concerned, such as matters of righteousness, faith, love, humility, and justice, than with academic achievement per se. It is the essence of this spiritual directive that we seek to advance in this chapter.

Figure 4.1 is designed to highlight how time spent in reading or studying helped the biblical characters identified to acquire vital knowledge of their role as spiritual leaders and enabled them to complete the assignments they were given successfully. This list is in no way making a judgement that other established spiritual leaders in the Bible never read. Those appearing in this list are chosen because there is clear evidence provided in the scriptures about their actual participation in the exercise of reading or study. The resources or material they read, and the nature of the effect such activity had on the capacity they possess and services they delivered, are recognised in it.

The life and ministry of each of the characters identified offer something important about what is possible when one reads the resources integral to personal ministry calling and responsibilities. By reading the law of the Lord, they each acquired a deeper understanding of their duties and how they were to discharge them effectively. As such, they demonstrated devotional obedience to the directives given by the Lord God; impacted their generations and those from other nations, eras, and realms; and they secured the commendation and promotion of the Lord God.

There is much that we could learn from these and other bible characters, if we are prepared to invest time to read their stories and study their life and ministry, within the context of their times and seasons. By doing this, we would locate ourselves at the right place to grow and develop our capacity for Ministry and increase our chance of achieving outcomes that can be laid alongside theirs in the Lord's presence.

The place of importance that we are encouraging spiritual leaders to identify and press towards is that which helps in recognising the uniqueness of the ministry roles which are to be fulfilled in partnership with the Holy

Spirit, who determines them (1 Cor. 12:4–11). Suppose this is not one of the critical insights gained at the early stage of our spiritual journey into leadership. In that case, the Ministry will become congested with spiritual clowns who parade before people but lack dynamism to effect change for God's glory. Younger leaders sometimes adopt the style of prominent leaders but have nothing to show in power and effectiveness, at the place of delivery. Learning to skip across a stage or merely uttering specific phrases does not constitute a unique spiritual ministry. To do that is to become a clown and not a spiritual leader. To adopt the discipline of prayer and that of reading and to study the scriptures, as practised by prominent spiritual leaders, would be a worthy investment in growing and developing personal capacities for human welfare and the glory of God.

	Figure 4.1		
	Growing and Developing Personal Ministry Capacity through Reading and Studying (as Modelled by Selected Biblical Characters)		
Bible Characters	**Reading/ Studying Activity**	**Key Resources Engaged**	**Effectiveness in Ministry**
Joshua	Joshua 1:8	The Book of the Law (Deuteronomy)	He discharged the duties of his office, divided the land amongst the tribes (Joshua 22:1–9)
Josiah	2 Chronicles 34:14–28	The Book of the Law (Deuteronomy)	National Reformation: • Public repentance • Restoration of true worship (2 Chron. 34:29–33)
Daniel, Hananiah, Mishael, and Azariah	Daniel 1:3–4	The Law of the Lord (Deuteronomy), Chaldean literature	Advisors in the royal courts of Babylon; Governor to Darius in the kingdom of Medeia Persia (Daniel 1:17–21; 3:28–30, 6:1)
Jesus	Luke 4:16 Matthew 5:17	The Torah, the Law of the Lord, the Prophets	He accomplished all that the Father gave Him to do. (John 17:4)

Peter	Acts 6:4 2 Peter 3:15–16	The Torah, the Law of the Lord, Prophets, Paul's letters	He offered credible spiritual truths to his readers. (2 Peter 3)
Paul	Acts 22:3	The Torah, the Law of the Lord, the Prophets	He fulfilled numerous missions and is credited with the authorship of 14 of the 27 books of the New Testament served.

In ending our discussion on time in the Word of God as a vital strategy for capacity expansion, we wholeheartedly recommend the work of Tom Barnes. His reflection on Proverbs 2:1–5 encourages believers to come to the Word of God as persons searching for treasures. He states,

> Early on in the book, one of the basics in which these young disciples were instructed is that of treasuring the commandments of the teacher and seeking wisdom "as for hidden treasures" (2:1–4). In other words, with the same tenacity that we might search for a lost wallet, full of money and credit cards, in a football stadium, so we are to hunt for wisdom from God. The result will be that the treasure hunter will come to understand the fear of the LORD and find the knowledge of God (2:5). Here, most likely, there is the same that the wisdom seeker will not only know what the fear of the LORD is, but also how to come to it and why it is important.[51]

It is as disciples of Jesus Christ that we desire to understand the call to Ministry and grow in conformity to His revealed identity. In offering witness on His behalf to the world around us, we come to the Word of God as persons seeking for treasures. By the Word, we grow our capacity to fear the Lord and become more intently engaged in delivering the vital Ministries to which He assigns us. Therefore, this desire puts us in the valued position to serve the Lord and His people with more significant insights and a deeper understanding of the core objectives that serve as motivation for our efforts and sacrifices.

---

[51] Tom Barnes, **Every Word Counts**, (Darlington, England: EP Books, 2010), ps. 17-18.

Figure 4.2
Personal Reading Evaluation Grid
Growing and Developing Personal Capacity for
Productive Living and Ministry through Reading

Instruction: Consider your reading habit for the last month. Then use the following questions and statements to help you evaluate it.		
1.	What were your main motivations (reasons) for participating in the exercise of reading for the period you reflected on?	
2.	Identify all the sources you read for the period you reflected on.	
3.	List some of the benefits you have gained from the reading you have done for the period in question.	

Instruction: Consider your reading habit for the last month. Then use the following questions and statements to help you evaluate it.		
4.	Provide a brief description of how your reading informs your capacity for Ministry.	
5.	Account for how your motivations for reading relate to the benefits you have gained from it.	
6.	How might you use the learning you have acquired from reading to support those you serve to grow and develop their God-given capacities?	
7.	Evaluate the responses you provided to all of the above and then account for the insights gained from this exercise, which you can use to grow and develop your capacity as a Minister in the Church of the Lord Jesus Christ.	

2. Prayer: A Vital Means for Capacity Expansion and Development

Of the fundamental importance of prayer, as a process by which divinely bestowed capacities are expanded and developed, the renowned Andrew Murray's classic work *With Christ in the School of Prayer* offers a vital testimony that demands our time and attention. The importance of this classic composition, which accounts for the value of prayer as a strategy for expanding and developing spiritual intelligence and warfare tactics amongst believers, can be ascertained from the following synopsis taken from the preface he wrote for this work in 1885.

> Of all the traits of a life like Christ's, there is none higher and more glorious than conformity to Him in the work that now engages Him without ceasing in the Father's presence—His all-prevailing intercession. The more we abide in Him, and grow into His likeness, the more His priestly life will work in us mightily, and our life becomes what His is, a life that ever pleads and prevails for men.[52]

Murray's words are more than theological rhetoric. All the facets of the life of Christ bestowed to all who believe in Him are made quite evident. Still, they offer so much that we would do well to grasp and own for ourselves. The value of authentic discipleship which affords conformity to Christ Jesus in character (Rom. 8:29) is one such facet. Expansion and development in the service of sharing the saving knowledge of God and Christ to the nations (John 17:3), as we are commissioned (Matt. 28:19–20), is very much in view. These are two spiritual gems that Murray advances for the adorning of all who are yoked together with Jesus (Matt. 11:29–30). Our participation in the discipline of prayer is of immeasurable value in our striving for Christlikeness. Prayer, then, is how conformity to Jesus is obtained and effective service to humankind gets achieved. In essence, Murray's invaluable book teaches how prayer serves to build the capacity of Christian disciples and facilitates and grows their influence to prevail in the presence of the Lord God, on behalf of humankind. The knowledge that secures our entrance into the presence of the Lord God

---

[52] Andrew Murray, *With Christ in the School of Prayer* (Massachusetts: Hendrickson, 2007), 1.

and obtains positive responses to requests that benefit others is in fact the invaluable truth that Murray's work on prayer endeavours to publish among believers, spanning many centuries.

Importantly, Murray's work on prayer, which points to the composite value of prayer as a means for capacity expansion and development among disciples of Jesus Christ, is not the first of its kind to be produced. Others who lived centuries before his time have produced works of a similar nature. For example, St. Athanasius's account of the Egyptian-born third-century desert father St. Anthony, dubbed "the father of Christian monasticism", is one such person. He highlights the prominent role prayer played as a means of increasing spiritual capacity for victorious living and effective service throughout his life, ministry, and discipleship journey, and in the face of the many supernatural temptations he faced.[53] To successfully overcome the sabotaging strategies of demons, he instructed those who looked to him for instruction and guidance in the ascetic life:

> Hence, too, the necessity of much prayer and ascetic discipline that one may receive through the Holy Spirit the gift of discerning spirits and may be able to know about them—which of them are less wicked, which of them are more so; and what special interest each one of them pursues and how each is rebuffed and cast out.[54]

Interestingly, the name and functions of demons are not ascertained through extensive study but much prayer. This is in no way disregarding the valuable works that learned and experienced spiritual warriors have composed.[55] Indeed, many insights are available from reading them that can affirm experiences that are new to many of us, while aiding the development of an enriching language that can be used to articulate all that is revealed and experienced. The value of this is measured by what it offers to enhance the growth and development of all who are involved in the work of Jesus' Church. However, it is the time spent in prayer before

---

[53] Robert T. Meyer, *St Athanasius: The Life of St Anthony* (New York: Newman, 1978), 39.

[54] Ibid., 39.

[55] Lester Sumrall, *Demons: The Answer Book* (New Kensington: Whitaker House, 2003); Canon Ken Gardiner, *The Reluctant Exorcist: A Biblical Approach in and Age of Scepticism* (Herts: Instant Apostle, 2015).

the throne of God that best fits us with what is needful and necessary for effective, devotional, and sacrificial service among the human community (John 15:7–8; Acts 4:23–31). The Holy Spirit alone can identify such vile spirits and reveal their character, disposition, and skillset in perpetrating evil in the earth. Curtailing the activities of unclean spirits and dislodging them from the places they inhabit and from which they advance their wickedness, requires the revelation of the Holy Spirit. This revelation is downloaded to sanctified hearts that are given over to the service of much prayer and other vital spiritual disciplines, such as fasting and reading the scriptures. Increasing capacity for effectively engaging in spiritual warfare was experienced and advanced by St Anthony as a product of much prayer.

A more contemporary example is Donald Coggan, the former archbishop of Canterbury. He offers further insight into the role prayer plays in the expansion and development of believers' capacity in his riveting book *The Prayers of the New Testament*. The vitality of the message he shares can be perceived from the outset of the book, which sets into motion the valued role of prayer in increasing and developing believers' capacity for the delivery of Ministry that positively affected the lives of many during the first century AD. Notably, he highlights that it was through much prayer that Jesus had His capacity replenished to minister to those who continuously press in upon Him. He sets this forth not as a commentary located in some ancient historical context but as the standard to which contemporary Christians aspire to continue what he accomplished and commissioned His followers to strive for as a spiritual value. He stated in his commentary on Mark 5:25–34 concerning Jesus, "Being very man, it 'took it out of Him' to minister to the needs, spiritual, mental and physical, of those who daily pressed in on Him."[56] He further remarked, "He could not carry on a ministry of constant self-giving without such renewal."[57]

The essential spiritual renewal to which Coggan gave much attention pertains to a life habit of prayer. He cited Mark 1:35, Mark 6:46, and Luke 6:12 as indicatives of Jesus's prayer habit, which kept His power capacity at an optimum level so that He was in a state of readiness to expose and cast out unclean spirits and release their victims into the liberty of the sons

---

[56] Donald Coggan, *The Prayers of the New Testament* (London: Hodder and Stoughton, 1967), 15.

[57] Ibid., 15.

of God. Coggan encapsulated the vitality of prayer as a means of capacity expansion when he offered the following summation of his reflection on Jesus's prayer habit and its impact on the ministry He delivered to humankind.

> This would suggest that the right background for special prayer in an emergency is the steady habit of daily prayer from which our knowledge of God grows. He who knows God in the intimacy gained from daily intercourse will not lack guidance when, in an emergency or faced with a weighty decision, he turns to Him for special direction.[58]

We cannot afford to overlook or minimise what is possible through prayer to expand and develop the capacity we have received from the Lord. As so clearly and positively stated by Coogan, those who make prayer a life habit will increase in the knowledge of God. This is knowledge that the children of God require for victorious living and effective Ministry engagement in spiritual service. Our trust in the Lord, our awareness of ministerial strategic operation, and the vitality of the invaluable communion that relationship with God in the Spirit affords will undoubtedly undergo transformation and expansion by whatever revelation God gives of Himself. Prayers offered in sincere faith that are grounded in the Word of God are always prevailing. Time spent in daily intimate communion with God the Father is promised with the reward of an evident public manifestation of divine might (Matt. 6:6).

However, in the teachings of Jesus and the writings of the first apostles, we find the foundation that inspired and underpinned that which they have shared, out of the context of their own seasons of Ministry (a season that happened amongst their own generations). While there is much to be gleaned from the works produced by such heroes and heroines of the faith, we are promised much more from the source of the cannon of the inspired Word. Therefore, it is to the teachings of Jesus and the letters of the apostles that we now turn to discover in a new and refreshing way how God intended that we should grow and develop the capacity that He bestowed upon us through the gift and ministry of prayer.

---

[58]   Ibid., 16–17.

Of the increase and development of our capacity for effective service in the Church of the Lord Jesus Christ and amongst the people of the world, who are yet to be delivered from the powers of the kingdom of darkness, the gift of prayer is given by the Lord God. It is lamentable that the community of believers has suffered extensively from an underdeveloped and ineffective Ministry, even though God has blessed us with the gift of prayer for the increase and maturity of divinely bestowed capacities. John Maxwell appear to have discerned the heart of this matter when he states, "Despite God's promise of the power of prayer to change us and our world, many Christians never tap into it. They come to Christ but then live beneath their privileges."[59]

A similar lamentation can be raised in respect of the degree to which the members of Jesus's Church, within post-modern society, are involved in delivering the Great Commission. Despite being directed by the Lord Jesus to "pray the Lord of the harvest to send out labourers into the harvest" (Matt. 9:38) and to go and "make disciples of all nations" (Matt. 28:19–20), many are still content to remain inside the "house of pleasure"' while the harvest goes to ruin. The idea of being in God's kingdom and becoming His heirs and joint heirs with Jesus (Rom. 8:17) is hijacked from its context and used to fuel carnal ambitions that contravene the critical message of conformity to the portrayal of the suffering Christ. Self-denial and cross-bearing (Matt. 16:24–27) do not appear to feature in the theology of salvation that some Christian leaders advance through the ministry they build around themselves. The practice of stripping the message of the Gospel of the kingdom of God to construct a theology of prosperity that views the sufferings of Jesus Christ as an activity that secures redemption but not an example for His disciples (John 15:18–20; 1 Pet. 4:1–2, 12–16) is not only fallacious but extremely dangerous!

Misinterpreting and misapplying the contents of the Holy Scriptures presents a real issue for the Church. It undermines the expansion and development of spiritual capacities. It renders gifted and misguided Ministers ineffective in the Church's service to all who seek examples of authentic biblical disciples to emulate in a world riddled with disingenuous leaders. Besides, it transposes the bearers of such errors into "spiritual icons"

---

59   John Maxwell, *Partners in Prayer* (Nashville: Thomas Nelson, 1996), 10.

that offer flawed representations of what it means to become conformed to the image of God in Christ Jesus.

It is most interesting that Dela Quampha reports revealing yet troubling insights in his valuable work that interrogates the ethical foundation underpinning and informing Pentecostal Ministerial living and serving in Ghana. His work highlights some of the core features of those comprising a fraction of Ministers who appear determined to breach the teachings of the Holy Scriptures in pursuit of wealth and fame. He observes:

> Moreover, there appears to be a worrying trend amongst Pentecostal leaders, by which moral concerns receive less preference than they did with their Holiness movement progenitors. The contemporary Pentecostal emphasis on the success and prosperity motif suggests that, to them, enjoying the temporary benefits of relating to the divine take precedence over the eternal dividend of moral transformation. Furthermore, it appears that many of these church leaders, public opinion, social status, and reputation take precedence over character issues and moral decency.[60]

The yeast of this flawed theology serves as the premise from which many believers direct their requests to God for things they think will increase their influence over others, accentuate opinions of themselves, and maximise unrestrained carnal pleasures. Such efforts are invariably met with disappointment primarily because they fail the proof test of authentic prayer outlined in the epistle of James (James 4:3). However, the cry of spiritual deprivation and abject poverty is frequently heard among the people God called to be involved in the Church's service and those she serves. The persistency of this duplicitous disposition, which appears entrenched among many who occupy leadership offices in Jesus's Church, is one factor that affects holistic productivity for the benefit of all. James spells this out in clear terms to facilitate correction from evil practices and to encourage alignment with God's will, as outlined in the Holy Scriptures (James 1:5–8).

God's non-responsiveness to faithless prayers should not come as a surprise to anyone who reads the Holy Scriptures from a place of humility

---

[60] Dela Quampha, *Good Pastors, Bad Pastors: Pentecostal Ministerial Ethics in Ghana* (Eugine, OR: Wipf and Stock, 2014), xvi.

and true faith. Understanding God's holiness, of which the scriptures speak most profoundly and boldly, teaches the searching heart that God is not in the business of propping up individuals' ego and breaching His Word because someone prays long prayers and cry many tears! Jesus's teaching in Matthew 6:5–7 demonstrates that everyone who holds to such a view is deluded. Because faithless prayers secure nothing but silence from the Lord, it does not affect capacity expansion and development. Emptiness, lack, and vindictiveness constitute the harvest that faithless prayer produces.

Personal spiritual lack is not just a concern for Ministers of God who experience it; it is a community issue primarily because it has a knock-on effect on the people over whom such Ministers preside. The lack often reported among many who engage in spiritual services, has led to the manipulation and exploitation of the very people who should be receiving services that bring about deliverance and enrichment in the Church of the Lord Jesus Christ.[61]

Curtailing the lack that is generally spoken of amongst church communities and silencing the bitter lamentations that have become such a characteristic feature of their operations is a task Ministers of grace are required to manage forthwith! But this becomes possible when such leaders rediscover and apply the essential teachings outlined in the inspired scriptures about the vitality of prayer as a means of capacity expansion and productivity for life and service. Accepting and appropriating the fundamental teachings that are offered to all believers, through the inspired scriptures about prayer, brings into sharp focus the activity of praying. Learning about prayer and praying are two sides of the same coin. Learning how to pray is just as important as learning about prayer and how it can bring about a vital increase in the capacity we possess in grace.

The example of the early disciples offers many insights concerning how we might begin to approach delivering effectual and fervent prayers. After observing Jesus engaging in the ministry of prayer and witnessing the excellent results He obtained, the disciples asked Him to teach them how to pray so that they too would know within themselves, and also within their delegated ministry assignments, the intrinsic efficacy of prayer.

---

61   Marie M. Fortune, *Is Nothing Sacred?* (Oregon: Wips and Stock, 1999); Deirdre Offord, *The Betrayal of Trust: Addressing the Impact on Congregation When Leaders Abuse Their Positions* (Cambridge: Grove, 2009).

In response to their request, the Lord Jesus pointed out some generally concealed pitfalls to sincere and effective spiritual prayers and then went on to outline how His disciples could deliver prayers in utter simplicity and faith (Matt. 6:5–15; Luke 11:1–4). It is this subject that Pete Greig developed in his excellent book *How to Pray*.[62]

The Prayer Analysis Grid: A Toolkit for Capacity Expansion and Development

The following prayer analysis grid offers a list of scriptures that we are encouraged to use as an aid for engendering personal transformation and the inculcation of the spiritual disposition required for meaningful participation in praying prevailing prayers. It also seeks to provide a framework for assessing the type of requests we generally make in prayer before God our Father. Although this toolkit is in no way comprehensive in its intention to foster growth and development through prayer, it does serve the critical purpose of encouraging believers, especially established Ministers of grace, to become proactive in evaluating the effectiveness of time spent in prayer. This evaluation exercise also seeks to highlight the intrinsic value of prayer in shaping the character and significance of the Ministry in which each believer engages. In essence, we designed this grid specifically to expose the expansion and development that is possible in respect to our various capacities, whenever we who are justified by faith in Jesus Christ (Rom. 5:1–2) pray effectual and fervent prayers (James 5:16b–18).

The prayer analysis grid is designed with three sections. The first section contains a series of scriptures, each focusing on specific teaching about prayer and the central place it should occupy within the believer's life and service. It seeks to offer some benefits to clergy and lay leaders who commit themselves to undertake this exercise in good faith.

The second section is concerned with the intrinsic evidential features of capacity increase and development as contained in the various portions of scriptures selected for this exercise. Therefore, Ministers are encouraged to read and reflect on the chosen passages and discern the inherent growth and development features that are expressly stated or inferred from their contents.

---

[62] Pete Greig, *How to Pray* (London: Hodder and Stoughton, 2017).

The third and final section of the prayer analysis grid provides exercises for reflecting on which particular aspects of your capacity are most likely to be developed through careful meditation and analysis of the expansion features that can be discerned from the passages of scripture identified in the exercise.

We have completed the first of the following two grids to illustrate how the exercise might be done. The second grid is for you to complete on your own or with others in a small-group setting. This exercise intends to impact capacity expansion and development through a planned bite-size Bible study activity. Acquiring a deeper understanding of the Word can only contribute to the growth and development of one's capacity. As one increases knowledge in the substance of God's Word, faith will increase for more valiant service in prayer for the welfare of the saints (Eph. 6:14–20) and the salvation of those who are blinded by the devil (2 Cor. 4:3–4) and living under his evil influence (Eph. 2:2).

Figure 4.3
An Example Prayer Analysis Grid

Scripture References	Intrinsic Features of Increase and Development	The Nature of the Capacity Impact Most Likely to Be Produced
Matt. 6:5–14	"The Father's presence waits in the secret place for those who seek after Him." "The Father knows the things one is in need of even before one asks (prays)." "Your Kingdom come; your will be done on earth as it is in heaven."	Believers' faith, confidence, and trust in the Lord stand to grow in the light of the self-revelling knowledge of God which is given in the secret place This revelation about prayer expands the knowledge of a believers' importance in the Kingdom and the courage expressed in living and service A more significant opportunity and access to all that is required for life and service

Scripture References	Intrinsic Features of Increase and Development	The Nature of the Capacity Impact Most Likely to Be Produced
Matt. 6:5–14	"Give us this day our daily bread." "Forgive our debts, as we forgive our debtors." "Deliver us from evil pathways and the evil one."	The entirety of a believers' life—inclusive of the personal and missional—stand to be positively affected for more significant effect in living and service This knowledge produces confidence before God and boldness and courage before the enemy The totality of a believers' life and missional work are intended to be positively affected by this provision of grace
Matt. 18:15–20	"Whatever you bind on earth will be bound in heaven, and whatever you loose on earth will be loosed in heaven." "Again, I say to you, that if two of you agree on earth concerning anything that you ask, it will be done for them by My Father in heaven." "I am in the midst of the two and the three who gather in My name."	Increased confidence in managing situations that threaten the purity and unity of the faith Intending to bolster assurance and faith and to inspire courage to manage threatening situations responsibly Intending to encourage caution and increase faith for working in accord with divinely stable processes

Scripture References	Intrinsic Features of Increase and Development	The Nature of the Capacity Impact Most Likely to Be Produced
John 14:12–13	"The works that I do will be done by those who believe in Me because I go to the Father." "Whatever you ask in My name, that I will do that the Father may be glorified in the Son." "If you ask anything in My name, I will do it."	The basis for working effectively in the kingdom of God is faith in Jesus Christ; this allows believers to access that which the Father has willed for His children on the earth Jesus provides a solid guarantee that believers' prayers will be answered because He is present with the Father at the time of asking The assurance that builds faith and encourages believers to make requests in prayer is reinforced by the emphasis Jesus placed on His presence with the Father and His willingness to reward our faith
John 15:5–8	Abiding in Jesus Christ, who is the fullness and the substance of all that is needful for growth and development Receiving and holding protectively the vital instructions and promises which Jesus gave	Anticipating increase in general and specialist knowledge from being intimate with the Living Word—growth in faith capacity Increased confidence in discerning the will of the Lord through the spoken Word and more significant influence before the presence of the Father in prayer: growth in ministry effectiveness

Scripture References	Intrinsic Features of Increase and Development	The Nature of the Capacity Impact Most Likely to Be Produced
John 15:5–8	Asking and receiving all that the spoken Word produces in desire within the soul, mind, or spirit Fruit-bearing on a cosmic scale is the expected result of a life that benefits from intimacy with Jesus Christ and all that He gave in instructions and promises	Increase in the spiritual competence required to glorify Father God: greater depth of experience in the delivery of worship to God the Father They offer a more significant body of evidence to both the galaxy of spiritual beings and humankind of one's authentic discipleship to Jesus Christ.
James 1:1–8	Ask the Lord to supply every lack that you discern The Lord is a generous, liberal giver of gifts Faith is the key for securing all that is lacking from God Identify and resist every feature of potential sabotage to faith and its promise of good things from the hand of the Lord	Expansion in invaluable spiritual information and strategies for self-management amidst hostile situations Maturing in the various competencies of the faith

Personal Developmental Exercise

Read the following passages of scriptures and then fill in their corresponding grids in accord with the following.

1. What potential recourses can be obtained from the following identified passages of scriptures that you can use to affect your capacity's expansion and development?
2. How can you use such expected positive resources to support those you serve to grow their capacity for victorious living and ministry effectiveness?

Scripture Reference	Personal Capacity Growth and Development	Facilitating Growth and Development in Mentees for Ministry Effectiveness
Mark 1:16–20		
Acts 4:23–31		

Scripture Reference	Personal Capacity Growth and Development	Facilitating Growth and Development in Mentees for Ministry Effectiveness
Acts 4:23–31		
Eph. 1:15–22		
Phil. 4:8–9		

3. Peer-Conversations: A Necessary Tool for Growing and Developing Capacities for Effective Ministerial Service

An age-old strategy that has much to contribute to increasing and developing Ministers' capacity is peer conversation. Although we regularly engage in this type of activity, we do not always recognise it as a meaningful way by which we grow our respective capacities. Peer conversations do not constitute a substitute for supervision. It is an entirely different learning and development strategy that can produce knowledge that is different from that generated within supervision. This is not to say that the understanding and development that is possible through peer conversations is superior to or better than that which is obtained from supervision. The fact of the matter is that these strategies produce different types of knowledge that contribute to expanding and developing the capacities that Ministers of God possess. Besides, supervision generally happens within a structured hierarchical frame.

In contrast, peer conversation happens in collegial relationships that are not conformed to the strict process to which supervision generally conform. Those who engage in peer conversations are doing so not because it is a requirement of their employment. Therefore, we can view peer conversation as an activity that happens outside of the boundaries of formal supervision arrangements. Because peer conversation is informal and without structural constraints, it allows Ministers to choose those they wish to converse with without the restrictions of organisational obligations. Ministers can engage in conversation with others outside denominational boundaries without feeling restrained.

To alleviate any discomfort or anguish that one may experience at the very mention of the idea of peer conversation, we must offer some additional guidance concerning its operational nature. We do not use the term *peer* in this book in the general restrictive sense to which we are all familiar. We do not intend that it should be understood in the sense of having an age-restrictive nature. Peer conversation can happen intergenerationally.

Therefore, the term *peer* speaks about Ministers of God sharing a common calling to serve in the Church of the Lord Jesus Christ. We are mindful that there are ranks, offices and positions, and varying degrees of experience amongst all who are currently involved in the service of the Lord's Church. The demarcations that such a structure tend to impose can sabotage the growth and development of the respective capacities in operation. More senior Ministers and those occupying the higher ministerial ranks could have restricted their personal and pastoral development primarily because of the elitist disposition they may (unknowingly) bring to the Ministry. Those who carry such attitudes demonstrate, by their behaviour, that they are not receptive of the contributions of others who do not serve at their level, have offered, or are wanting to contribute. In some cultures, it would be considered an insult for Ministers occupying a lower rank to presume to initiate a conversation or ask a question that may have the appearance of a critique of something that a more senior Minister may have said or done.

The type of peer conversations that we are proposing here for capacity growth and development is primarily concerned with mutual Ministerial engagement that is not restricted by ranks and offices and positions. It allows for more senior leaders to be challenged in respect of their, sometimes, outdated, and ineffective methods of service delivery, through informal conversations with younger Ministers, who often are in the know of the day-to-day operations at ground level. In a peer conversational setting, younger ministers have the opportunity to benefit from the insights and wisdom which more senior Ministers have gained through experience. In essence, this proposed engagement pathway could provide a real chance of growing and developing capacities because those dreaming dreams and receiving visions (Joel 2:28) share out of the riches of their spirit without inhibitions but as fellow labourers in the service of the Lord. They genuinely desire each other's development and effectiveness in Christian service, much more than building monuments in one's name!

Unlike supervision, in general peer conversations can be unstructured and unscheduled. By this, we mean they do not follow a set pattern in terms of start and finish time, recording of topics discussed, and guidance offered. They do not demand the high level of confidentiality intrinsic to supervision; hence, peer conversations can occur almost anywhere— on the telephone, through letter writing, by email, by video chat, and face-to-face. One of the beautiful things about peer conversations is that they can happen during mealtimes or even while travelling together. The promise of acquiring knowledge that can aid personal capacity growth and development through conversation with fellow Ministers, outside of the confines of supervision, is most encouraging. The issues and subjects facilitated by this process of expanding capacity are dependent on the openness and confidence of those who choose to engage. Anything and everything can be discussed without the constraint of prejudice and structural boundaries. This is one of the benefits of this process.

The learning that such conversations promise for those choosing to be involved in peer-conversation is unquantifiable. Time spent in conversations between Ministers of grace, whether face-to-face, video chat, phone, or even by email, contribute significantly to the growth and development of all who are willing to speak candidly but wisely, and listen with a critical and understanding ear. Taking additional time to carefully evaluate the substance of such intentional conversations, in which Ministers invest themselves in good faith under the leading of the Holy Spirit, can only result in mutual capacity growth and development. Given such possibilities, we recommend that Ministers of grace—clergy and laity—avail themselves to participate in peer-conversation. This engagement is not with the motivation to compete but to explore perceptions and ideas for discovering truths that will expand and develop the divinely bestowed capacity for affecting more significant outcomes in biblical spiritual ministries.

4. Growing and Developing Ministerial Capacities through the Medium of Supervision

The body of Christ is designed to utilise the principle of supervision for collective growth and productivity in worship and service. The Lord assigned leadership roles within families, businesses (Deut. 6:1–7; Eph. 6:1–9), ministry groups and church communities (Eph. 4:10–16; 1 Pet. 5:1–7). This demonstrates that He intends to give us precious things that far supersede the carnal intentions of propping up personal egos and securing compliance from those who have seen themselves as lesser beings in the Church of Christ. Receiving power, position, and opportunity through grace has to do with offering a service to others that is supervisory in nature. Being an example and offering a context where others can learn and grow in becoming more effective fellow labourers in the work of Jesus's Church, are the objectives that fulfilling leadership in families, businesses and church ministries seeks to achieve.

Supervision is, therefore, one of the essential processes by which children of God who are engaged in the delivery of the Ministry of Grace can grow the capacity they possess and affect positive outcomes in "fruit production" (Matt. 5:16; John 15:8) while heightening personal satisfaction in service (1 Thess. 2:19–20). Many individuals who are involved in spiritual service do not engage in supervision. As such, they miss out on the vital learning that the process, when properly managed, can deliver. Even where the process is established as an essential activity of an individuals' Ministry function, it does not always yield positive results, especially when those who are tasked with its delivery use it as a means to exercise personal power. When Ministers misuse authority like this, it results in the abuse of individuals, exploitation of position, and reduction in the level of organisational success and development that is possible. Hence, abusive supervision is an area of importance within organisations that has generated extensive research.[63] Although this research is predominantly undertaken within social contexts that do not overtly share the values and operational processes intrinsic to spiritual movements, such as the Christian Church, the findings they generate have applications for the power relationships within Church communities and organisations.

However, when supervision is delivered with positive developmental intentions and biblical spiritual motivation, it allows for the critical appraisal of the specific service one offers. It also provides a general overview of one's performance in Ministry against previously determined objectives, which provides for accountability and the development of those who engage in its process. Importantly, whilst those who receive adequate supervision are apparent beneficiaries of its operations, those involved in its facilitation also stand to benefit.

Supervision provides a space for Ministers who engage in the process to grow in their awareness of the ministry style they adopt and utilise when engaging in ministry delivery. In terms of the language code generally used in service delivery, additional valuable understanding is also afforded during supervision. Critically reflecting on how Ministers view themselves, within the context of the roles they fulfil and the services they deliver, is an area of importance that supervision makes possible. The effects of congregational demands and the responses they give to the services they receive on the image and popularity of Ministers within the immediate and broader context where

---

[63] Bennett, J. Tepper, "Consequences of Abusive Supervision", *Academy of Management Journal* 43, no.2 (2000), 176–190, DOI: 10.2307/1556375.

they serve are other vital areas pertinent to capacity growth and development which supervision caters. The capacity growth and development value inherent to such an exploration may be identified in the answers that the following questions generate: What gets done whenever ministry is delivered? How do these vital elements impact ministry delivery? In what ways does the dynamic interactive process of ministry affect the Minister's identity? These are some of the crucial explorations that supervision provides Ministers who are serious about personal and ministerial capacity growth and development, within an operational structure that holds integrity, accountability, and the pursuit of holiness as priority objectives in the mission of winning souls for Jesus Christ.

After establishing and reflecting on some of the understandings that defining supervision generates, we want to further reflect on two additional points we raised in the introductory comments to this section. We hope these will broaden the scope of supervision as a capacity expansion strategy for Christian Ministers. These points are supervision as a discipline of immense value in the personal and professional lives of those who serve in the Church of the Lord Jesus Christ and abusive supervision. The second of the two is a sabotaging force that works against the holistic learning and developmental agenda that is intrinsic to believers' maturity in spiritual affairs and the advancement of the redemptive mission of Jesus's Church in the earth.

A. Supervision—What Is It?

In general, supervision is recognised as a process or as an event. Supervision as a process has to do with foremanship or management that is surveillance oriented. It is hands-on, in that it is always observing, assessing, checking, and measuring what others are tasked to do within the context of work. This kind of understanding about supervision is akin to what J. Peach and N. Horner describe as "a management activity singularly concerned with overseeing staff's productivity and progress".[64] In this regard, supervision is believed to have "connotations with direct control, discipline and surveillance".[65] It is axiomatic that supervision, as defined

---

[64]   J. Peach and N. Horner, "Using Supervision: Support or Surveillance?" in M. Lymbery and K. Postle, eds., *Social Work: A Companion for Learning* (London: SAGE, 2007), 228–239.

[65]   Ibid.

here, is very much about patrolling and policing people and the work they do. This supervision method seeks to ensure that the objectives of the service that is delivered and the role of supervision, which is invariably different, is always achieved. This is not necessarily a positive thing for those being supervised and the organisation in which they work, as this manner of supervision "can become a tool of accountability and efficiency"[66] instead of one that enhances professional development, improves practice, and maximises service provision.[67]

Another definition of supervision focuses on "supporting, developing and motivating",[68] and it "relates to the concept of a 'learning organisation', defined as: 'organisations where people continually expand their capacity to create the results, they truly desire, where new and expansive patterns of thinking are nurtured, where collective aspiration is set free, and where people are continually learning to see the whole together'".[69]

This understanding of supervision is more in keeping with viewing the process as a planned activity. Supervision as a scheduled activity is a meeting between two people, of which one fulfils the designated role of supervisor (generally, someone who holds a position of greater responsibility and possible learning and understanding), and the other, the defined role of the supervisee (which is the one receiving supervision). Although this is a scheduled event, we do not view it as a stand-alone event that has no connection or relationship with the work or service that those involved in the process of its delivery represent. However, it directly feeds back into the service of the organisation through the expansion and development of specialist knowledge and the validated experience of those receiving supervision.

The idea of supervision as a process of directing or overseeing someone's performance or watching over to maintain order[70] is not what we are advocating here. We recognise that power relations are intrinsic to supervision and inform its function within the context of Jesus's Church, and from which it receives

---

[66]   Joyce Lishman, "Personal and Professional Development", in Robert Adams, Lena Dominelli, and Malcolm Payne, eds., *Social Work: Themes, Issues and Critical Debates, Second Edition* (Houndsmills: Palgrave, 2003), 103.

[67]   Ibid.

[68]   ACAS, www.acas.org.uk.

[69]   Peter M. Senge, *The Fifth Discipline: The Art and Practice of the Learning Organization,* (New York :Doubleday/Currency, 1990), 3.

[70]   *Collins English Dictionary,* 1669.

no respite or exemption. We believe that supervision within the spiritual context of the Church does not advance the idea of policing those who receive care from overseeing Ministers. As such, we welcome the fact that the lived experiences of those delivering ministry within a hostile world are viewed as essential to the process of supervision. It therefore forms a necessary part of the plan that is explored within supervision. Therefore, supervision is not restricted or blinkered by the need to encourage conformity to the fundamentals of the faith. Within the Church context, supervision facilitates agreement in pursuit of holiness because it provides the essential bedrock within which Christian identity and its operational missional goals are anchored.

Furthermore, what supervision offers is the support Ministers require to identify critical ministerial processes and find pathways to discover vital meanings within current personal struggles and associated ministry challenges. Such discoveries are in accord with biblical discipleship. They are built upon the foundations of Christ Jesus, the apostles, and the prophets (1 Cor. 3:11; Eph. 2:19–22) and are necessary for validating the result, which is conformity to the image of God, as so clearly revealed in the person of Jesus Christ (John 1:14, 18; Rom. 8:29). They also generate an intimate understanding of spiritual services that bolster faith in God and courage to remain faithful to the ministry.

The goals supervision aims to achieve, whenever it is done with the integrity implicit to the context of Jesus's Church, are highlighted in D. Mearns and Mick Cooper's work. Although the specific context within which these goals are identified is the person-centred approach to counselling and psychotherapy, their vitality is pursued through supervision in any service context and applicable to Christian Ministry. They postulate:

> Within supervision, there is a tendency for the work to go in one direction: ongoing practice is examined and issues arising are explored so that they may facilitate further personal development that feeds back into future practice. This is great—it is real learning from ongoing experience, well supported. However, it also makes sense to make the ongoing developmental agenda explicit within supervision.[71]

---

[71] D. Mearns and Mick Cooper, *Working at Relational Depth in Counselling and Psychotherapy* (London: SAGE, 2005), 155.

The points of importance raised here by Mearns and Cooper are very applicable to the process of supervision that we are advocating for Ministers who are engaged in the delivery of services in the Church of the Lord Jesus Christ. It is the experience of engaging in the Ministry that forms the plan for supervision. This is not one-dimensional but multifaceted. It allows for exploring experiences and challenges, which feeds right back into and influences ongoing personal growth and development and the Minister's continued engagement in service delivery. Making the developmental agenda explicit in supervision ensures that personal and professional development for improving practice, enhancing service, and maximising productivity, is specified and always outlined in clear terms. Even specific issues such as ministry activities and responsibilities are discussed within its parameters because they are vital aspects of work fulfilled by many leaders in the Church of Jesus Christ. This is vital because it serves to prevent detours and potential sabotage of the supervision process.

B. Abusive Supervision: A Sabotaging Force against Capacity Expansion and Development

It may appear contradictory to speak about abusive supervision as a prominent feature of current Ministerial operation in the Church of Jesus Christ. The reality of abuse should never be a prominent feature in the life and function of the Church when we consider that perpetrators of abuse received the Holy Spirit, who administers the love of God within the inner life of believers (Rom. 5:5). Besides, members of Jesus's Church are God's fellow workers (1 Cor. 3:9). There is no leeway provided within this holy life-giving operation for the carnal expression of abuse. Jesus admonished every disciple who desires and aspires to occupy high offices to be the servants of others and give perpetuity to the excellent example of servitude He masterfully portrayed while He walked in the flesh among humankind (Matt. 20:20–28; John 13:1–17). Paul echoed this vital spiritual directive in Galatians 6:1–2 and Ephesians 5:1–2, as did Peter in 1 Peter 5:1–7, for our learning and as an established sign before our eyes. The exact opposite of what is commanded by Jesus Christ and reiterated by the apostles has become the behaviour that inflicts many wounds upon the members of Jesus's Church.

Abusive supervision is identified, in research, by the following behavioural manifestations: "public criticism, loud and angry tantrums, rudeness, inconsiderate actions, and coercion".[72] This list is by no means exhaustive but is sufficient for illustrating some of the features that stand in direct contrast with the spiritual directive Jesus gave to His Church in Matthew 20:25–28. We accept that such behaviours are negative by the social conventions that inform and govern acceptable reciprocal respectful human relationships. Evaluating such actions within the context of the communion of Jesus Christ and the Holy Spirit most certainly brings into focus a much deeper level of the incredulity such manifestations would attract when displayed by those occupying the ranks of commissioned witnesses of the Lord Jesus Christ. To anticipate such a response is not unreasonable in the least. It is good that those who operate outside the boundaries of biblical spiritual ministries have an awareness of the standard that characterises the life of the people of God and can raise questions about any duplicitous expression of ideas or behaviours that our faith community may demonstrate before their presence. The good works that believers demonstrate before the watchful eyes of the world and its citizens generate a worshipful response that celebrates God's presence as Father and life-giver, amongst the community of faith (Matt. 5:13–16). Correspondingly, the harmful behavioural conduct that is contrary to biblical spiritual standards leaves people in doubt and darkness about the authenticity of the faith, evokes blasphemies that grieve God's heart, and creates barricades to the ministry of the gospel amongst those who are in sin and darkness.

At its core, abusive supervision serves as a sabotaging force that negatively affects the expansion and development of capacity. It does this by the various ways in which it makes gifted and capable people frustrated, helpless, and alienated from the place of work.[73] These effects

---

72   R. J. Bies, "Interactional (In)justice: The Sacred and the Profane", In J. Greenberg and R. Cropanzano, eds., *Advances in Organizational Behaviour* (Stanford, CA: Stanford University Press, forthcoming).

       R. J. Bies and T. M. Tripp, "Two Faces of the Powerless: Coping with Tyranny", in R. M. Kramer and M. A. Neale, eds., *Power and Influence in Organizations* (Thousand Oaks, CA: Sage), 203–219.

73   Blake Ashforth, "Petty Tyranny in Organizations: A Preliminary Examination of Antecedents and Consequences", *Canadian Journal of Administrative Sciences* 14 (2009), 126–140, https://doi.org/10.1111/j.1936-4490.1997.tb00124.x.

of abusive supervision absorb the energies needed for investing in growing and developing capacity. They serve as distracting parasites that blunt the sharpness of the mind and blur the soul's vision by transforming the joy of learning into an experience of anguish that can leave vibrant people intellectually starved, creatively emaciated, and productively impoverished.

Abusive supervision does not merely affect gifted and talented people negatively; it also prevents the growth and development of whole organisations and communities. Because of the divisive nature of abusive supervision, organisations are negatively affected due to "absenteeism … and reduced performance".[74] The links between abusive supervision and various psychological distress indexes are also troubling because even the milder manifestations may engender significantly high social and financial costs for organisations.[75] Such adverse implications are inevitable. This is expected whenever workers' morale becomes eroded and the stimulus for growth and development, which are viable productivity and satisfaction indicators, is curtailed and eroded by abusive supervision.

C. Biblical Spiritual Model of Supervision

Because the Church of Jesus Christ is a spiritual entity grounded in Judeo-Christian theology, it is needful and necessary that there is an established Biblical Spiritual Method of Supervision (BSMoS) to which those engaged in the delivery of service in the Church of Jesus Christ should participate. To depend on other disciplines, such as social work (SW) and person-centred counselling (PCC) to define the parameters and the vital skills-set that inform the nature of the supervision that Ministers of grace receive, is qualitatively impoverished and spiritually undermining. Because SW and PCC are humanistic in their theoretical foundation, practice orientation, and goals pursuit, they are inadequate supervision models for Ministers of Grace whose identity and service are defined and informed by the Holy Spirit (John 3:3–5; Acts 1:8; 1 Cor 12:4–11). Having a biblical spiritual model of supervision (BSMoS) is advantageous for safeguarding Ministers of grace and the Ministry's integrity on the whole. Importantly, it is a service determined by Ministers in

---

[74] Tepper Bennett, "Consequences of Abusive Supervision", *Academy of Management Journal* 43, no. 2 (2000), 178–190.

[75] Ibid.

partnership with the Holy Spirit for the welfare of Ministers whose identity and service are dependent on the Holy Spirit. Therefore, it provides Ministers with a context within which to experience the efficacy of the dynamic workings of the Spirit in facilitating capacity growth and development through the process of critical reflection. This facility is needful for effective service delivery within the current socio-political and religious climate of the world.

When we speak about a BSMoS, we refer to the role inspired scriptures plays in determining the process that supervision should take, as well as the objectives pursued whenever it happens. We used the term *biblical* to promote the critical role the Word of God plays in informing the character of BSMoS. Also, we used the concept *spiritual* to account for the Holy Spirit's position as the chief agent in BSMoS. We recognise and revere Him in His role as the Helper who comes to us from God (John 15:26) to teach us about the kingdom of God and to provide leadership and guidance in all that is true (John 14:16–17; 16:12–15). The Spirit's empowerment for the delivery of service for the glory of the Lord Jesus Christ and God our Father is very much in view whenever we speak of BSMoS (Acts 1:8).

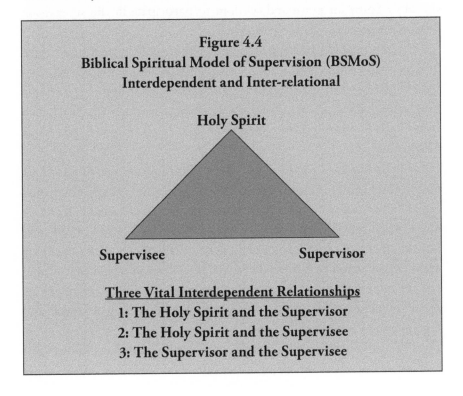

Figure 4.4
Biblical Spiritual Model of Supervision (BSMoS)
Interdependent and Inter-relational

Holy Spirit

Supervisee   **Supervisor**

<u>**Three Vital Interdependent Relationships**</u>
1: The Holy Spirit and the Supervisor
2: The Holy Spirit and the Supervisee
3: The Supervisor and the Supervisee

BSMoS is wholly different from other supervision models because it happens through the Holy Spirit's empowerment and under His leadership. Furthermore, it is grounded in the content of inspired scriptures. It considers the entirety of all that constitutes the life and ministry of Ministers of grace and not just who they are in relation to the objectives of the work the Holy Spirit enlists them to fulfil. As illustrated in figure 4.1, there are three distinct but interdependent and inter-relational encounters that happen simultaneously whenever a BSMoS becomes established. The relationship between the Holy Spirit and the supervisor constitutes one of the three interdependent relationships within BSMoS. The second interdependent relationship is that which exists between the Holy Spirit and Supervisee. The third interdependent relationship is that which exists between the supervisor and supervisee. The indispensable person in these relationships is the Holy Spirit. As He brings conviction to the heart of the one receiving supervision, He affords discernment to the supervisor so that the best possible counsel is offered to resolve and overcome any challenge brought to supervision. Therefore, both the supervisor and supervisee depend on the Holy Spirit for grace and wisdom to participate in the supervision process intentionally and responsibly.

The personal spiritual and emotional welfare of Ministers are essential aspects of any supervision undertaken within the process of the BSMoS. Hence, Ministers are expected to account for the health of the relationship they share with their spouses. How they manage other integrity-laden issues such as money, power, and trust also forms essential aspects of BSMoS.

Supporting a colleague within the supervision context to reflect on their spiritual and emotional state is vital if signs of fatigue and exhaustion are to be spotted to prevent emotional and physical burnout, lapses in judgement, and inadequate service. In addition to such positive outcomes, all the other varied and potentially destructive consequences that may eventually arise can be discerned and curtailed through advanced planning and the establishment of safeguarding measures. This kind of knowledge serves to increase the vigilance required for protecting personal and organisational integrity.

The idea of organised supervision is treated as unimportant by some Ministers. Anecdotal information indicates that Ministers who consider the marks of a successful Ministry to be personal power and influence, popularity, money, external praise, and a large following sometimes frown upon supervision and overly rely on captivating charisma, academic achievement, or family connections. However, giving the required attention to this seemingly insignificant element in the life and service of Ministers can prevent spiritual bankruptcy and all the shame and carnage with which it is generally associated.[76]

How Ministers manage their spousal relationship, personal finances, and the other critical areas within which integrity failings are widely reported[77] can affect capacity development either positively or negatively. Whenever Ministers of grace give appropriate regard to their call to holiness and spiritual services, the kingdom of darkness recedes in influence and territory, and souls are added to the Church of Jesus Christ. However, personal failings in the areas noted above will reduce capacity production in the pulpit and before the world at large. Compromised Ministerial integrity not only reduces credibility within the home before spouses and children or in the pulpit before fellow believers, but it also weakens the stance of Ministers in spiritual warfare before the enemy. Whenever this happens, the entire realm of spiritual operation that concerns Ministers becomes subject to shame. Their homes, the congregations which they lead, and other types of ministries as the case may be, can suffer the very same catastrophe that we read about in Genesis 3 concerning Adam and Eve and their descendants.

The story of King David's wicked deeds, which is narrated in 2 Samuel 11–12, provides an account of the various ways in which sin can impact the life of Ministers of God concerning their credibility and the influence they have within the following fields of importance: their household (Ammon, Tamar, and Absalom), those employed in their service (Joab), and amongst their enemies (the Philistines). There is much to learn from this story. We

---

76 Siw T. Innstrand, Ellen M. Langballe, and Erik Falkum, "The Longitudinal Effects of Individual Vulnerability, Organisational Factors, and Work–Home Interaction on Burnout among Male Church Ministers in Norway", *Mental Health, Religion and Culture* 14, no. 3 (2011), 241–257, https://doi.org/10.1080/13674670903470621.

77 Warren Wiersbe, *The Integrity Crisis* (Nashville: Oliver Nelson, 1991); Johnathan Lamb, *Integrity: Leading with God Watching* (Nottingham: Inter-Varsity Press, 2006).

recommend that you take time to consider the value of David's choices and their implications for your life and the ministry you are called and empowered by the Lord to deliver in His name amongst your community.

Sin breaches our spiritual defence and provides access to the devil and his hordes whenever Ministers reject God's revealed will. Because sin is, in effect, an act of disobedience or the rejection of the laws of the Lord God, scripture tells us that the devil takes advantage of those who are inclined to live in such a way and therefore dominates them to the point of enslavement (Eph. 2:2).

Therefore, engaging Ministers in conversation about their spousal relationship and the management of other vested areas of life and ministry to which integrity directly relates is not about hunting for dirt. Instead, it is about protection, accountability, and the opportunity to support other church family members to grow in awareness and knowledge of self and others. It enables the development of vital strategies for safe and appropriate behavioural expressions that are in accord with biblical directives, enhancing positive reports of the faith amongst all who are involved in its promotion on the earth.

D. An Example of a Biblical-Spiritual Model of Supervision

A BSMoS to which we can aspire is found in Luke 10:1–24. In this example, we observe the Lord Jesus appointing seventy disciples and sending them out in pairs to achieve some clear ministry objectives. The first responsibility Jesus asked them to manage was praying to the Lord of the harvest to send labourers to reap the ripe and ready harvest. Second, He gave them directions concerning the mental and character disposition they were to adopt and display. They were to view themselves as lambs going to do work in a world filled with people who possess wolf-like tendencies. They were then instructed not to take any resources with them; this was the third responsibility they were to manage on this mission. Fourth, He directed them to remain in the house wherever they entered and found reception. They were to be content with whatever food they received and not move from one house to another. Fifth, Jesus instructed the disciples to heal the sick people of the city and preach the good news of the imminence of the kingdom of God. Sixth, He urged them to shake the town's dust off their feet with a pronouncement of judgement in those places where residents rejected them and the message of salvation that they preached.

Upon their return from discharging their duties, they provided a one-dimensional report about their experience to Jesus. The disciples celebrated the fact that demons were subjected to them as they ministered in His name. They perceived this to be a high point in their participation in Ministry. Although Jesus affirmed them as persons empowered to exercise authority over Satan and his brood of vipers and scorpions, He challenged them to give attention to their personal salvation, which was the real objective of His coming to earth and also that of His calling on their lives, to bear witness of Him to the nations of the world (Matt. 28:19–20; Acts 1:8).

There are many important points of learning to be found in the above case study. Some are enumerated below for your consideration.

1. The context and the contents of the ministry to which the disciples were called, empowered and directed to deliver, are highlighted.
2. We have the actual supervision, which consists of the following elements:
   a. An account of the experience of the delivery of ministry and how it impacted persons and communities
   b. An appraisal of the experience gained and the value it produced for those who were involved in ministry
   c. Jesus's affirmation of those who participated in the delivery of ministry
   d. Jesus clarified what the real objective was in ministry, for those who engaged in its delivery
   e. Jesus celebrated God for having reserved such power and opportunity for those upon whom they were now bestowed

Supervision that allows for an evaluation of the service we deliver and a critical appraisal of the assessment that we bring to them is necessary for ensuring that the knowledge gained from any experience in Ministry would yield fruits of righteousness whenever we share them with others. This is one of the vital objectives we surmised from the reflective process through which Jesus brought the disciples. Because the discipline of critical reflection is not a standardised practice amongst many involved in the delivery of ministry in Jesus's Church, having set and regular supervision will undoubtedly help alert Ministers to the inherent benefits it affords for growing and developing capacities.

As we have presented in the supervision case study assessed above, invaluable knowledge is available through supervision that helps Ministers better discern between inappropriate and appropriate ministry goals and between transient and eternal values. Demons may be subjected to us as we deliver ministry in the name of the Lord Jesus Christ; however, this does not guarantee entry into the eternal Kingdom of God (Matt. 7:21–23). In supervision, Jesus cautions those who were quick to use ministry successes as collateral for gaining entrance into God's eternal Kingdom to re-evaluate any such thinking in the light of Luke 10:1–24. This is just an example of the benefits supervision promises whenever it is done correctly.

Template for Delivering a Biblical Spiritual Model of Supervision

The following is a template that we recommend for delivering BSMoS. This template is not cast in stone. It is a suggestion for those who are without a supervision structure. It can be used as designed or modified to facilitate supervision in the ministry context where one serves. The template requires the listing of information about the organisation within which supervision happens, the scheduled time of supervision, and the Ministry designations of those engaged in its delivery. This is intended to promote accountability and instil confidence amongst those who engage with the process, whether as supervisor or supervisee.

Accountability is critical because it safeguards those who serve in the Ministry and the people who receive the ministries for which the Church is responsible. Accountability structure allows for establishing a checks and balances system that promotes appropriate use of power and opportunity amongst people who are aware of the human propensity to be selfish and self-protective. The value of accountability in biblical spiritual service cannot be overemphasised in a climate where the church is proven to operate a silence culture that protects the perpetrators of heinous crimes against vulnerable worshippers.[78] Furthermore, accountability also safeguards the Church as an organisation. It positively aids the promotion of the Gospel of the Lord Jesus Christ and the kingdom of God in a world that is generally hostile to all that is heavenly and holy.

Engaging in biblical spiritual supervision designed and administered by those selected to give leadership to an organised group of Holy Spirit ordained and empowered servants is critical to establishing and regulating defined processes and an established structure that everyone can rely on. Without a carefully thought-out strategy, those who deliver supervision and those who receive it would have a real challenge determining the objectives to be achieved whenever they meet. The same can be said about the absence of a structure of accountability. In other words, who must provide oversight for those delivering supervision, and to whom can those receiving supervision appeal should they feel that the service they receive is not positive and beneficial to them? These are just some of the potential challenges that clearly defined processes and an established accountability structure advertised and robustly administered with sensitivity and integrity, can avert for all concerned.

The second half of the proposed supervision model is concerned with the substance of the supervision. It presents a list of subject areas explored in supervision to encourage and affect capacity growth and development. We have identified these with brief commentary throughout the remainder of this subsection.

---

[78] Ron O'Grady, *The Hidden Shame of the Church: Sexual Abuse of Children and the Church* (Genever, WCC, 2001).

Figure 4.5
School of Ministerial Excellence
Supervision Performa

Name of Organisation: _____

Date of Supervision: _____

Name of Supervisor: _____

Office/Role of Supervisor: _____

Name of Supervisee: _____

Ministry Designation: _____

Supervision Agenda:

I.   Pray for the success of the supervision

II.   Setting the agenda for the supervision

III.   Personal physical and spiritual health

IV.   Personal spousal and family relationships (where applicable)

V.   Power management in ministry

VI.   Safeguarding personal integrity in life and ministry

VII.   Personal financial probity

VIII. Ministry role/responsibility: issues and challenges

IX.   Rest, relaxation, and recovery

X.   Personal developmental needs/action plan

The Rationale for the Ten Areas of Enquiry Outlined in the Proposed Supervision Structure

I. Prayer

Prayer should bathe everything we do in life and Ministry. Through prayer, we receive the knowledge of God and the vital wisdom and power required for listening to and accepting, with discernment and compassion, those who come to supervision with concerns and challenges from their involvement in spiritual service. Praying for the Holy Spirit's leading for the effective management of the process of supervision is a requirement that none of us should flaunt—considering that the growth and maturity of all concerned are the objectives being pursued. Therefore, prayer must be offered in all sincerity and full submission and dependence on the Holy Spirit.

Spending time in prayer sets the hearts of those engaging in the supervision process in a state of reliance on the Holy Spirit to shed light on every dark situation and expose latent carnal desires and intentions. Because prayer provides insight for resolving problems, and courage and wisdom to recognise and talk through subjects that may be shrouded in shame or embarrassment, it must have prominence in the supervision process. This may be obvious to some yet unrecognised by others. It can be one of the vital aspects of supervision that is taken for granted because those involved in delivering supervision have become reliant on the techniques of explorative conversations and learned helping strategies. Making prayer a definite priority in the supervision process demonstrates submission to the Holy Spirit and dependence upon His illuminating and revealing might to minister love and care to those who come to such an experience in brokenness and great need.

II. Setting the Agenda for the Supervision

It is generally a good thing to determine the content of the supervision just after time in prayer. This is prudent because those involved in the supervision would then be more sensitive to the Holy Spirit's work in the inner life. While it is crucial to ascertain what issues are uppermost in their minds and ensure that these are set in order of priority, the last eight subjects or themes presented in the above supervision structure should not be set aside. These are generally the broad critical areas that generate much concern for those involved in delivering ministry within the Church and the wider community. Establishing a plan helps to give structure to the process and prevents unnecessary wandering and misuse of time.

III. Physical and Spiritual Health

Though not advisable nor beneficial, we know that several Ministers continue to be involved in the delivery of ministry while they are physically unwell. Many even continue in service, although they are emotionally and mentally ill. Various motivations underpin such practice, which comes with adverse effects, primarily because it generally affects congregations' spiritual health. A lack of personal insight is sometimes one of the causes of this kind of practice amongst Ministers. An inability to recognise when emotional and physical fatigue is setting in is that which we highlight here. Besides, immediate and prolonged personal socio-economic considerations are sometimes the real motivating factors that cause Ministers to continue in service when a reasonable timeout for rest and recovery would produce more enduring benefits for all concerned.

This lack of insight is equally evident amongst lower-ranked Ministers as well as those who supervise them. Supervising Ministers can become so programme-orientated and task-driven to the extent that the actual emotional and physical welfare of those they supervise gets overlooked in their eagerness to meet targets. Therefore, a holistic approach to training is required to upskill Ministers across the ranks if this lack is to be expeditiously remedied. Only those who serve at the helm of the Church can make this happen. This can be done either by planning and delivering a programme for all Ministers on its initiative—particularly those currently serving in a supervisory position—or securing a certified and credible external agency's services.

It is unwise for a physically unwell Minister to continue to delivery ministry. This practice could exacerbate any condition they may have and put them out of service for a prolonged period. This could even lead to Ministers losing their lives in an untimely manner. Preventing the untimely death of Ministers must be avoided at all costs. Curtailing suffering is what a Holy Spirit directed service seeks to achieve, and the supervision process could be the channel where this noble goal is achieved.

Being spiritually unfit cannot be treated with the same leniency given to a situation where a Minister is physically unwell. Determining what would make a Minister spiritually unfit for service should not be debated between the supervisor and supervisee. This cannot be the case seeing that both are working to a set of directives drawn from the inspired scriptures and the legal context in which they deliver their respective service. These directives are generally outlined in a church's statement of purpose, articles of association, constitutional documents, administrative policy and procedures, and employment contract, where such are in existence.

Discussing the subject of a Minister's physical, mental, and emotional health, within supervision, requires spiritual and emotional sensitivity, established and strong relational ties, and a good grasp of counselling skills. Realising that the real objective is not to find fault but to offer support where required is necessary for the success of the process, the growth and development of the Minister, the prosperity of the church in which he or she serves, the enhanced maturity of the supervisor, and the integrity and success of the organisation.

IV. Personal and Family Relationship

A Minister's family can be one of his or her most significant assets in finding success and prosperity in the Ministry. It can also be the means by which whatever he or she tries to do in ministry fails. Family is not just an institution that a Minister happens to be a part of; it is a vital element in a Minister's life and service. Such is the vitality of family as a spiritual entity that God has given it a place of high priority in the inspired scripture. From the beginning of the scriptures, the family and its vital importance in God's creation are highlighted as central themes.

God established the family to work in partnership with Him to manage the earth (Gen. 1:26–30). We are informed about its most basic form being that of a man and his wife (Gen. 2:18–25). Throughout the process of time, God gave additional information in scriptures about how a man and his wife ought to live in a family (Eph. 5:17–33) and how they are to care for the children their union produces (Deut. 6:1–25; Eph. 6:1–4). He informs us in scripture that a man needs to provide for his family (1 Tim. 5:8). Furthermore, He teaches us that disagreement between a man and his wife can lead to spiritual poverty, and as such a practice seems to have the power to nullify their prayers before the presence of His throne (1 Pet. 3:7).

Ensuring that the Minister's family is highlighted for discussion within the supervision process is a point of importance that we cannot overemphasise. Enquiring about the health of the Minister's family so that support can be offered where concerns become evident, is in keeping with the BSMoS. The support required may be much more than prayer. Should this be that case, much should be done to help manage the situation insofar as resources will allow.

V. Power Management in Ministry

Exploring with Ministers within the process of supervision, how they understand and use their office's intrinsic power, allows for accountability for Ministers and safeguarding for all concerned. Many church workers serving in the high offices of bishops and pastors are reported to abuse their power and the trust implicit in their office.[79] Even those who served in other offices not regarded with the same level of prestige ascribed to bishops and pastors, such as Sunday school teachers, youth workers, and church van drivers, are reported to be abusers of power.[80] Exploring the management of power as an integral part of supervision keeps the subject of accountability in the main and heightens the level of vigilance in which Ministers need to be operating.

Therefore, as an essential aspect of the supervision process, the case of power management in ministry is one that the relationship structures at play within church communities and organisations make evident. The church is organised in a structural format and operates a top-down approach to power management. This organisational and operating structure demands that much attention is given to how delegated power is

---

[79] Galloway and Gamble.

[80] Carolyn Holderread Heggen, *Sexual Abuse in Christian Churches and Homes* (Eugene, OR: Wipf and Stock, 1993).

managed. The urgency for doing this has also been heightened where the church and its operations are confined to a cultural context that is rigid in its understanding and approach to utilising power. How persons with limited power or those without power are treated by the powerful in the Church of the Lord Jesus Christ should be of concern to all involved in the delivery of Christian service. According to the example of the Lord Jesus Christ, those involved in the Ministry are directed to serve with humility and use their influence to secure and advance the welfare of the poor (Phil. 2:1–4; 1 Pet. 5:1–4). This then is the standard to which we should all conform, in the service we render, whether in the pulpit, on the street, or the context of planned supervision.

VI. Safeguarding Personal Integrity in Life and Ministry

Overcoming the Darkside of Leadership,[81] which is for persons who serve as Ministers in the Church of the Lord Jesus Christ, has at its heart the mission of safeguarding personal integrity in both life and Ministry. Gary L. McIntosh and Samuel D. Rima use the stories of many prominent secular and spiritual leaders who failed to recognise and effectively manage their dark side to promote the value of proactivity in safeguarding personal integrity in life and service. Their explorations of a constellation of failed leaders discovered numerous pitfalls that ailed those who were either too arrogant or self-assured to avoid them. One such pitfall is most evident in the following passage: "Leaders who need to have success to validate themselves are driven to acquire these things and are willing to pay virtually any price to do so."[82] Where there is a lack of awareness of the nobility of the identity encouraged by scripture and affirmed by the Lord God, Ministers can find themselves left to find identity in things or achievements. It is not the Lord God that such Ministers seek to please but the insatiable carnal desire they are yoked to unnecessarily. Rest is available in the Lord for all who have laboured and become laden with the burden of disappointment that comes from seeking to cultivate identity and prominence through the fallacy of self-indulgence (Matt 11:28).

---

[81]   Gary L. McIntosh and Samuel D. Rima, *Overcoming the Darkside of Leadership* (Michigan: Baker, 2007).

[82]   Ibid., 20.

Walking in step with the Holy Spirit is not empty theological rhetoric. It is a directive given for maintaining a walk of holiness and victory living in a world where "the flesh" is very much a force against which Ministers must contend (Gal. 5:16–18). Consequently, everything infused with spiritual value is earmarked for extinction, primarily because they intrinsically carry revealing and restraining components that are not in accord with carnal pursuits. These values are generally sacrificed to achieve whatever the thing is that they feel will secure for them the elusive satisfaction and stardom they think they need to belong.

The BSMoS advanced, which we promote in this book, allows for exploring desires such as those discussed in *Overcoming the Darkside of Leadership*, with the expressed intention of supporting Ministers to cultivate a sense of intentional proactivity in developing and implementing personal safeguarding strategies. This will help protect the vital integrity that gives their lives and ministry the security and power required for promoting the mission of the Church within a hostile world.

VII. Personal Financial Probity

Financial mismanagement is one of the areas in which it is reported that Ministers demonstrate an evident weakness,[83] so we believe it should be identified as a subject for discussion in the supervision session for several reasons. It is not our intention to collude with the sinister cultural practice of naming and shaming or even that of sabotaging the success and prosperity of fellow labourers in the vineyard of the Lord Jesus Christ. Therefore, we declare at this juncture that exploring financial probity within supervision is not geared at discovering whether Ministers are succeeding or failing financially. The quest is of noble intention and not one of carnal abuse. It supports the development of a culture of holiness within which financial acquisition is encouraged without manipulation and exploitation, and its utilisation is open to unprejudicial scrutiny. The principle of accountability, which is a vital feature of both integrity and safeguarding, constitutes the underlying motivation for exploring financial integrity as a critical feature of the BSMoS.

---

[83] Wiersbe, *The Integrity Crisis.*

Exploring Ministers' financial management is a necessary activity which safeguards both Ministers and the witness of the Church in general. Providing the space for Ministers to account for how they manage their finances and that which belongs to the Ministry in which they serve can prove beneficial for all concerned. This helps Ministers to develop good money management skills that will contribute to effective personal stewardship. It also allows for an openness that will provide the required relevant support to help wherever issues or challenges are identified. The Church can better support and care for those who serve in the Ministry, especially in difficult times, when Ministers recognise the inherent value of talking about financial probity within planned supervision sessions.

What the BSMoS seeks to do for Ministers, where financial integrity is concerned, is dispel the mist that stifles and to break the silence that deafens so that the darkness of cultural taboos will be dispelled forthwith. Those who have suffered in silence for many years can now know the freedom available to all who trust in the Lord Jesus Christ for eternal salvation, once and for all.

VIII. Ministry Role/Responsibility: Issues and Challenges

This area of the supervision aims to help Ministers identify the central roles they fulfil and the core responsibilities intrinsic to them. This knowledge helps determine where physical efforts and financial aid need to be directed to prevent burnout, financial misuse, or poor investment. At times Ministers are involved in too many ministry projects and as a result find themselves thinly stretched to the extent that they produce nothing that is of lasting value. This can be likened unto the person who is seen as the jack of all trades but master of none. As no time is spent to wade through the various things that clamour for attention, many Ministers have become so involved to the extent that they are unable to identify the core responsibilities that they should be fulfilling. Supervision can help bring the required clarity so that Ministers can re-envision their core calling and take the necessary steps to become fully engaged for greater effectiveness in living and service.

IX. Rest, Relaxation, and Recovery

Supporting Ministers taking necessary rest for relaxation and recovery is very good for longevity and effectiveness. Holiday and leisure should be discussed as an essential part of the supervision process. Rest allows time for hurting and exhausted Ministers to heal and recover. Finding one's passion and the niche in which to deliver it is critical to prolonged success and prosperity in any field of service. Time of rest allows for Ministers of God to rediscover the authentic underlying passion for why they are in the Ministry. In this regard rest, relaxation, and recuperation descale the eyes and help clear away the cobwebs of lingering disappointments whilst realigning the mind and heart with the mission of Jesus's Church for which the Holy Spirit came to us from the Father to provide enlightenment and empowerment (John 15:26–27; Acts 1:8).

At this juncture, we must note that rest is necessary for healing the souls of Ministers of God. As physical exhaustion taxes the emotions and the body of those who serve in the Ministry of Jesus's Church, even so, rest allows for healing and recovery in these aspects of our personhood. Jesus was well aware of this fact and directed the apostles to take time out to rest, recuperate, and heal (Mark 6:30–32).

X. Personal Developmental Needs/Action Plan

Supporting Ministers through the supervision process to identify their learning and developmental needs is one way that Senior Ministers can help grow and advance those they supervise and the Ministry in which they are invested. The BSMoS is not geared at disempowering those receiving supervision, so promoting the growth, development, and advancement of those receiving supervision is an expectation of the process. Helping others recognise their learning and developmental needs and exploring avenues and options with them as to how these can be managed are some of the many positives that this model of supervision seeks to achieve.

Enquiring about the level and nature of preparation that Ministers undertake for managing the responsibilities identified above will bring awareness and allow for the development of necessary insights that will enable Ministers to better care for themselves. Asking Ministers to account for how they fulfil their role and responsibilities and allowing them space to account for any challenges encountered and how they manage them is vital to BSMoS. Encouraging them to detail whether predetermined objectives were achieved and what criteria they used to arrive at such conclusions are ways to promote the necessary skill of critical self-appraisal. Explore whether any learning needs have arisen throughout the course of one's ministry and discuss how those identified might be remedied through training, within a reasonable time frame. It is not just a positive thing to do; it is a biblical principle that Aquila and his wife Priscilla dutifully demonstrated in their dealings with Apollos (Acts 18:24–28). Weakness or deficit in ministry should never evoke mockery and ridicule from fellow labourers; instead, it should attract the interest and the involvement of mature individuals. This is the mark of a developing and maturing Ministry. It demonstrates conformity to the image of Jesus Christ. It provides irrefutable evidence that one is yoked together with Jesus Christ and is indeed a faithful disciple who lives in submission to His lessons (Matt. 11:29).

In summary, we want to highlight that significant growth concerning capacity expansion, is possible through supervision. Supervision is one area of capacity expansion and development that ministry teams should invest time and resources developing.

5. Reflective Practice and Reflection

Other professions, such as social work[84] and counselling,[85] view reflective practice or reflection in practice as a vital ingredient in the personal and professional development of those committed to serving within their respective contexts. The former is viewed and promoted as a critical aspect of the social work profession that allows practitioners to evaluate how their experience in practice relates to theory. In turn, it generates new knowledge that influences practitioners' development, both as persons and professionals. Although a similar idea is advanced in counselling, the additional ideas of reflecting on clients' various feelings

---

[84] Malcolm Payne, "Social Work Theories and Reflective Practice", in Robert Adams, Lena Dominelli, and Malcolm Payne, eds., *Social Work: Themes, Issues and Critical Debates, Second Edition* (New York: Palgrave, 2002), 123–138.

[85] Carl R. Rogers, *Client-Centred Therapy* (London: Robinson, 1951).

and emotions within the counselling process highlight how reflection is understood and used in counselling.

However, we understand that the two distinct manners in which reflective-practice and reflection are used in established professional contexts, such as social work and counselling, have relevance for Ministers within the practice of the BSMoS. The support supervising Ministers give to those they oversee is essential in cultivating the skills to, and habit of, critically reflecting on their ministry practice. These are the expected outcomes for an operational system informed by biblical theology, established code of ethics, and professional expectations. These can be measured by the invaluable knowledge generated and the improved effectiveness in Ministry that follows. Applying these principles generates additional knowledge and improves productivity that promotes the valued service Ministers deliver. There is no loss to be expected when Ministers of God exercise themselves according to these principles that promote the growth and development of divinely bestowed capacities!

Of all the processes that one may engage in regarding capacity expansion and development, reflective practice is one of the most challenging and intrusive of them all. Although reflection is essential to peer conversation and supervision, there is still another form of reflection from which Ministers can obtain many benefits. We label this authentic spiritual reflection.

The authentic spiritual reflection that we are here advancing differs from the previously mentioned examples, essentially because it is primarily concerned with the minister's inner world, as seen in the light of the Lord's presence. It is the experience of intimacy which divine encountering affords that provides the substance of that which is the content of the reflection that we are promoting here. What is at the heart of this reflection is not the level of faith that is exercised in response to the specific commands, which are outlined in the inspired scriptures, but an actual encountering of the Lord, on par with that of Abraham (Gen. 18) and Moses (Exod. 33–34). This is the most personal experience which is unmediated by another sanctified servant. The appraisal features or catalyst for analysis are not so much the impact one has on their audience, but the beliefs and attitude one holds concerning the Lord. This nature of this reflection can be quite disempowering and emotionally distressing and can be facilitated through others who have undergone a similar process. Of the many who have not gone through such a vital developmental process and the few who have, Janet O. Hagberg and Robert A. Guelich make the following critical comments:

> The sad truth is that many of these leaders (priests, ministers, pastors, bishops) have been through this stage themselves and have not allowed themselves to question deeply or to become whole. So many of those to whom we often look most naturally to for help are inadequate guides for this part of the journey. Those who have been through this stage themselves and may be specially trained in spiritual direction, spiritual formation, or pastoral counselling, are unique people and are to be sought out.[86]

Taking responsibility for one's development in the things of the Spirit cannot be overemphasised when we consider that not everyone who occupies a spiritual office is adequately prepared to positively manage the power and the responsibilities intrinsic to its function. Being through the mill, as it was, is necessary if one is to support others to undertake and complete the particular journey that they are now called to embark upon with the Spirit, with a more glorious trust in the Lord and greater humility in service to others. Taking time to seek out useful spiritual guides is vital to personal maturity in the things of the Spirit which are quite pertinent to our conformity to God's image, as revealed in the person of Jesus Christ. This also places upon church organisations and those who exercise leadership over their affairs the opportunity to work towards and encourage the development of that open, challenging, but caring culture where stalwarts in spiritual administration are trained to offer what is a most vital service to those who are now embarking upon specific Ministry pathways, and the broader population that we are established to serve.

6. Spiritual Tutelage

The process of Christian discipleship is wholly spiritual. This is because the kingdom into which persons who believe in the Lord Jesus

---

[86] Janet O. Hagberg and Robert A. Guelich, *The Critical Journey: Stages in the Life of Faith, Second Edition* (Salem, WI: Sheffield, 2005), 94.

Christ are called is spiritual. When we say that the Kingdom is spiritual, we are stating that the Holy Spirit is the agent by which individuals are called into the faith community. The Holy Spirit empowers all such persons with leadership capacity. He motivates them to express the significance of their new creation identity, in living and service, for the salvation of others and the ultimate glory of God. The specific biblical theology underpinning the truth of the spiritual nature of the kingdom of God is presented in clear terms in the inspired scriptures, for our learning. It is the means for affirming the spiritual identity and holy character which we possess in Christ Jesus. This also serves the purpose of providing the substantive and significant basis from which to serve our generation; all that we have received from the unfathomable bounty of the Father through the Holy Spirit (1 Cor. 2:9–12).

Notably, the identity of the very God who exercises sovereign authority over the universe and the kingdom to which those who believe in Jesus Christ belong is identified in the scriptures as incorporeal (John 4:24).[87] From the beginning, the incredible presence and works of the Spirit are registered (Gen. 1:2). Both the Old and New Testaments are replete with the exploits of the Spirit. Keith Warrington writes about the minimalistic view with which some believers perceive and hold the Spirit's identity. This improper view of the Spirit appears to be based on a misunderstanding of His presence and work in the Old Testament. He states, "The fact that when the Spirit is mentioned in the OT, it is in connection with his influencing only a small number of people also undermines his significance in the minds of many believers."[88]

Believers' failure to acknowledge the Spirit's Sovereignty in the Old Testament with appropriate reverence has affected how His presence and work are viewed therein. It has also prevented many from willingly embracing the truth concerning the spiritual nature of the kingdom into which believers have been called. This results in minimising our appropriate spiritual response to the evident natural developments and reductionism that characterises most of life, as it is understood and lived in

---

[87] Henry Clarence Thiessen, *Lectures in Systematic Theology* (: **William B. Eerdmans, 2006**), 75.

[88] Keith Warrington, *The Message of the Holy Spirit* (Nottingham: Varsity, 2009), 11.

the world. However, the nature and quality of our response to such realities should be different. This should offer evidence of the spiritual nature we possess because we are children of God, through faith in Jesus Christ (John 1:12–13), and possessors of the spiritual essence that been "born again of the Spirit" (John 3:3–5) provides.

The Old Testament offers excellent insights into the work which the Holy Spirit fulfils for human redemption; for example, see Isa. 11 and 61. However, in the New Testament, we find the more specific references of His converting and empowering activity and empowerment for spiritual consecration and service (John 3:3–5; Acts 1:8; Rom. 8:1–11; 1 Cor. 12:1–11; Gal. 5:16–18). This body of evidence points to the process of believers' spiritual maturing and the vitality of the kingdom into which we are called to live, serve, and have our being.

The Vitality of Spiritual Tutelage

The vitality of spiritual tutelage as a means for capacity expansion, as advocated here, is a call for believers to recognise and embrace the strategies which the Spirit employs, to facilitate the holistic development of believers for maximised results in living and service. The natural propensity of born-again people is to yearn for and desire the things of the Spirit (Col. 3:1). To follow the Shepherd of our souls, even as sheep follow the Shepherd, they have grown to recognise and trust (John 10:11–16), is not unusual for Christian disciples. Even so, the gifts (talents, abilities, capacities) bestowed by the Holy Spirit can only grow and develop under the guidance and tutelage that He provides.

i. Direct—Unmediated Revelations

Unmediated revelations are identified as one way that the Holy Spirit helps believers grow the capacity they have received. Unmediated revelations account for the Holy Spirit's work within believers' inner life and for which no other sanctified human vessels are involved. It is that vital work of revelation (1 Cor. 11:4; Eph. 1:15–19), which the Holy Spirit works in the inner life of believers, thus providing essential knowledge about the kingdom of God and the place and role we each fulfil within it, that is in focus here. This work of the Holy Spirit, which allows for the expansion of bestowed capacity, is expressed by Paul as "the power that works in us" (Eph. 3:20b) and "it is God who works in you both to will and to do of His good pleasure" (Phil. 2:13). Importantly, it is to produce beyond our asking and thinking that the power of God operates within the inner life of believers.

Let us also observe the explicit intent of the divine regarding the potential expansive nature of the work that the Holy Spirit fulfils within believers' inner lives. The message of Ephesians 3:20 is one that points to a blessing that is a double portion in its nature. The first is the granting of what is requested or thought about through the practice of meditation, which is predicated on the truth of the Word which the Holy Spirit deposits in the souls of believers. To receive what is requested will undoubtedly amount to our expansion in capacity. This is because we are receiving something that we did not previously possess. In addition to receiving what we have meditated on and requested, the Lord offers more, thereby expanding us in the capacity we possess for potentially greater effectiveness and productivity in whatever area of service we are engaged.

Therefore, we advance the idea of the Holy Spirit's unmediated work in the lives of believers for capacity expansion. This is concerned with an awareness of the will of God and our submission to its transformational and impactful work under the direction of the Holy Spirit. The merit of this teaching is also based on 1 Corinthians 2:6–16. God has willed much for the growth and effectiveness of His people in the earth, and it is the Holy Spirit who discovers all such blessing and reveals the same to all who live in ready expectation.

Therefore, walking in step with the Holy Spirit is critical if believers are to know and benefit from all that the Father provides in His will. Cultivating intimacy with the Holy Spirit is crucial to the growth and development of the capacity with which our new creation status is fitted. It does not benefit our lives only to read the scriptures and gain insights about the identity and historical works of the Holy Spirit. Having the prophetic statements about the works of the Holy Spirit fulfilled in our lives should be the expected and pursued ambition of all who currently occupy the realm of Christian discipleship. Knowing the Holy Spirit not as a character in world and biblical history but as the imminent and dynamic personal God is what 1 Corinthians 2:6–16 and Ephesians 3:20 is calling us to embrace in its expressive and substantive forms. The Holy Spirit has come to us from the Father (John 15:26), and not just as our seal for eternal salvation. Still, as the dynamic, creative, omnipotent, and immutable God, He came to facilitate our transformation and empowerment for victorious living over evil and Ministry effectiveness right here on earth. It is high time we tap into the reservoir of the Holy Spirit's empowering might and so move away from mediocrity to spiritual authenticity in both living and serving.

ii. Mediated Revelations

Being called from the world into the body of Jesus Christ has located us amongst people who are gifted by the Holy Spirit to offer mutually beneficial developmental services to each other. Ephesians 4:7–16 accounts for the developmental nature of the work which the Holy Spirit fulfils through the various offices that Jesus instituted in the Church. Through the respective offices of the apostles, prophets, evangelist, teachers, and pastors, the Holy Spirit delivers a vital ministry that engenders each believer's holistic development and maturity in Jesus' Church.

This is the mediated service of the Holy Spirit. It is so described because the Holy Spirit uses sanctified human instruments as agencies to positively inform and empower others for capacity expansion and effectiveness in living and service. The Holy Spirit's mediated work is accounted for in Romans 12:3–8, 1 Corinthians 11:7–11, and 1 Peter 4:10–11. This body of evidence endeavours to bring to our attention the potential for capacity expansion through the ministry that sanctified believers can share with others due to the various gifts and superior power that the Holy Spirit brings to bear upon each redeemed soul.

Timothy's relationship with Paul bears witness to the authenticity and effectiveness of the mediated revelation of the Holy Spirit in growing and developing capacity. Paul recounted the Holy Spirit's influence upon Timothy's faith formation and its expansion and maturity through the instruments of his mother and grandmother, and the pastoral and fatherly role he played in the process (2 Tim. 3:10–16). We can find many other examples in the scriptures, and the relationship Jesus shared with His disciples or apostles is very prominent. Collectively, these examples point to the vitality of the revelatory workings of the Spirit in the lives of believers. By them, we realise that the growth and development of the capacity for ministry and service of countless numbers of believers are positively affected through the surrendered lives of others. Therefore, it is not only through the direct work which the Holy Spirit achieves in the inner life of all who bow their knees before Jesus Christ that spiritual capacity gets developed. It is also through the ministry that the Spirit undertakes in partnership with other believers. It is the responsibility of all of us to be discerning and reverential of the Holy Spirit's presence and workings and be respectful and accepting of whatever strategies and instruments He chooses to use to encourage and facilitate the growth and development of the capacity we have received through grace.

An Evaluation of Personal Learning

Prompt	Personal Comments
1. **Evaluate the role of supervision in the growth and development of your capacity as a servant of God.**	

Prompt	Personal Comments
2. How might reflective practice contribute to the growth and development of your capacity as a child of God and a Minister in Jesus's Church?	
3. What is the role of the Holy Spirit in the development of your capacity as a servant of God?	
4. What insights can you draw from the role Paul played in contributing to Timothy's growth and development as a Minister of the Gospel of Jesus Christ, and how can these be applied to the relationship you share with your pastor or bishop?	

CONCLUSION

The most difficult challenge faced in producing this book was bringing it to a reasonable conclusion. This is the case because we realised, from what we have presented, that there are many other aspects to growing and developing capacity that can be highlighted and explored. However, we are grateful to the Lord for the grace He affords, and the privilege given to sketch some of the insights that have and continue to positively impact the growth and development of the capacity we received through grace. We believe the information shared in this book regarding the intrinsic nature of capacity, as well as the various strategies identified for facilitating its expansion and development for maximising potential and productivity, is inspired by the Holy Spirit and will yield good results for all who faithfully apply them.

As is the case with all who expect miracles from the hand of the Lord, it is not merely by hearing that we receive whatever He promised; it is by practising what is received in faith that miracles are obtained. Reading this book marks the beginning of challenging how we think about the capacity we have. However, for capacity expansion and development to be realised, each principle will need to become a recognisable character in one's living and service through the processes of critical reflection and faithful practice. This is the next challenge that we must resolve in our minds to commit ourselves to embrace without unnecessary delay!

The teaching Jesus gave in John 15:1–8 points to the spiritual objective of the expansion of the capacity which we received from God through faith in Him. Abiding in Him and allowing the word He shares to dwell within us constitutes a vital strategy for expanding and developing the capacity we possess in Him. It also identifies fruit production as one of the expected effects of expanding and developing our abilities. The glory of the

Father is the inevitable result of growing and developing divinely bestowed capacities. These are four glorious reasons for growing and developing our respective capabilities. Each of these reasons constitutes an aspect of the motivating might which underpins the call of God upon our lives. Besides, they each speak to the beautiful purpose for which God gave us the power of capacity, to demonstrate our significance as citizens of His Kingdom in living and service. This purpose is that of glorifying His name.

Receiving positive reviews for this book would help its promotion and any future work that we may produce. However, it is the testimonies of those whose lives are transformed and empowered to deliver effective ministries that change communities by applying the vital principles outlined in this book, which we anticipate above anything else. When these expected results are achieved, then the kingdom of God in its power and glory would indeed be with humankind.

As we close this book, which has stretched us in ways too numerous to mention here, we want to give you the last word. This takes the form of an appraisal of the critical statements you wrote at the end of the introductory chapter. The following grid provides the space for you to reflect on the extent to which your beliefs and thinking about capacity may have changed from the study you have undertaken, by reading the contents of this book and completing the exercises outlined in it. Finally, we have provided space where you can reflect on the extent to which the expectations you outlined at the start of this process have been met, exceeded, or otherwise affected.

No.		Previous Responses	New Responses
	Capacity Assessment Grid		
1	What is capacity?		
2	Do you think you have capacity? Please account for the capacity you have.		
3	Do you believe that your capacity is limited? If so, in what ways?		
4	Can capacity be increased? If so, what might you need to do to achieve this?		
5	Whose responsibility is it to increase your capacity?		
6	Is age a factor to capacity increase? Give explanations for your response		
7	Does capacity have a single or multidimensional structure?		

An Evaluation of Personal Expectations	
Stated Expectations	**Extent of Realisation**
1		
2		
3		
4		
5		
6		
7		

Lightning Source UK Ltd.
Milton Keynes UK
UKHW011814250521
384363UK00001B/20